Still
Green
and Growing

A Practical Spirituality for the Second Half of Life

Archbishop **Sylvain Lavoie** OMI

NOVALIS

D0558305

© 2019 Novalis Publishing Inc.

Cover design and layout: Audrey Wells
Cover image: Getty Images

Published by Novalis

Publishing Office
1 Eglinton Avenue East, Suite 800
Toronto, Ontario, Canada
M4P 3A1

Head Office
4475 Frontenac Street
Montréal, Québec, Canada
H2H 2S2

www.novalis.ca

Library and Archives Canada Cataloguing in Publication

Lavoie, Sylvain, 1947-, author
    Still green and growing : a practical spirituality for the second half of
life / Sylvain Lavoie.

ISBN 978-2-89688-559-6 (softcover)

    1. Spirituality--Christianity. 2. Christian life. 3. Self-actualization
(Psychology)--Religious aspects--Christianity. I. Title.

BV4501.3.L386 2019   248.4   C2018-905033-0

Printed in Canada.

The Scripture quotations contained herein are from the New Revised Standard
Version of the Bible, copyrighted 1989 by the Division of Christian Education of
the National Council of the Churches of Christ in the United States of America,
and are used by permission. All rights reserved.

We acknowledge the support of the Government of Canada.

5   4   3   2   1   23   22   21   20   19

Contents

Foreword

I look back and shake my head at the audacity of thirty-year-old Fr. Murray Chatlain accepting to spiritually direct a seventy-eight-year-old elder. She was a retired English professor –delightful, articulate and searching. I remember her saying, "I need at least twenty more years to get my life in enough order to go to God." It was about eighteen months later that God called her to the final journey, and in her mind she wasn't ready. Most of us die as unfinished symphonies. I find good teaching on Purgatory strangely comforting. But just because the reality will be like this for most of us does not mean it is not worth working on the symphony. This is the heart of Archbishop emeritus Sylvain Lavoie's latest book.

Archbishop Sylvain challenges us to work on our selves, and he provides us with some tools and mentors to do the work. He reminds us that growth in the faith journey is not like climbing a ladder. We are not to give into self-disdain or despair when we are flailing in the healing spiral or "falling upward." He states, surprisingly for me, that "the process of grieving is a lot like the process of forgiving." These are important notes in the work I need to do on my own symphony.

If asked to summarize Archbishop Sylvain's efforts in one word, it would be "courage." He blithely speaks of accompanying an abused person as she confronts her abuser. He orchestrates a gathering of a hurting community with a primary hurter. Even though the results are hard to measure, I am in awe of his courage to facilitate this work of healing. He models the courage to speak about the unspeakable and to trust God and the community to receive and encourage.

Thank you, Archbishop Sylvain, for your latest book. It is full of quotes and insights that challenge and inspire. May faith, self-awareness, intimacy and authenticity be key ingredients in our life and aging.

Archbishop Murray Chatlain
Archdiocese of Keewatin–Le Pas

Introduction:
Being Open to Transformation

A young boy asked his parents if he could
be alone with his newborn baby sister.
Curious, they left the door open
and overheard him say to her, "Quick, tell me
what God is like. I'm beginning to forget."

—Anonymous

Setting the Context

"**I**f you're green, you grow; if you're not, you rot."

That arresting statement came my way decades ago and has stayed with me ever since. It has served as a constant reminder:

To be human is to be in process, growing, changing, learning, open to new possibilities and realizing one's potential.

I believe it is John Cardinal Henry Newman who coined the phrase "To live is to change, and to be perfect is to have changed often."

In that light, I have been reflecting on how that continued growth and transformation is manifesting itself in the second half of my own life, begun some years ago. How is it unfolding – and how should it be unfolding? Realizing it is never too late to grow, I was eager to learn more, and desiring to share that reflective process, the journey of writing this book began. Names and examples have been altered to ensure anonymity unless permission has been granted to share a story.

At the outset, I want to mention that this is not an academic or scholarly work, but rather a practical, pastoral and somewhat personal guide to living a fuller, more rewarding life as we age.

I will unabashedly blend my own experience and reflections with the writings and teachings of Ron Rolheiser OMI, president of the Oblate School of Theology in San Antonio, Texas, and Richard Rohr OFM, founder of the Centre for Action and Contemplation in Albuquerque, New Mexico, both of whom are very knowledgeable in the area of the second half of life. For readers not familiar with these two gifted mentors who have consistently taught me so much and shed light upon my pilgrim path, this work may serve as an introduction.

Growth as a Challenge

Personal growth and human development are both an inside job and the work of a lifetime. For some people, this process can be threatening and filled with fear, leading to resistance to the very idea of change and shutting out any possibility of transformation.

I remember a sincere parishioner telling me, "God created us the way we are and that's the way we are supposed to stay!" A CEO of a company shared with me his frustration and challenge of dealing with some older employees who resisted any new ideas or practices, with heels dug in. As a self-protective defense against having to change, they tried to take some of the younger workers under their wing and influence them to think and act as they themselves did.

Joyce came to me with a predicament. Her husband, with whom she had six children, was an alcoholic. His doctor warned him not to drink anymore or he would die. Never having dealt with the roots of his addiction, yet afraid of dying, he switched to working compulsively. On the road with his job for a week at a time, he found other employment that kept him mostly absent when he was home. Joyce was at her wits' end, trying to raise their children on her own and wondering how much longer she could keep up as a "married single." Her husband simply refused to look within, to change, to actually begin to grow personally and spiritually.

Unrealized Potential

The Christopher Leadership Course on effective speaking, personal growth and self-confidence introduced participants to this story of the Changeling Eagle:

> A man found an eagle's egg and put it in the nest of a barnyard hen. The eaglet hatched with the brood of chicks and grew up with them. All his life the eagle did what the barnyard chicks did, thinking he was one of them. He scratched the earth for worms and insects. He clucked and cackled. And he would thrash his wings and fly a few feet into the air. Years passed and the eagle grew old. One day he saw a magnificent bird far above in the cloudless sky. It glided in graceful majesty among the powerful wind currents, with scarcely a beat of its strong golden wings. The old eagle looked up in awe. "Who's that?" it asked. "That's the eagle, the king of the birds," said his neighbour. "He belongs to the sky. We belong to the earth – we're chickens." So, the eagle lived and died a chicken, for that is what he thought he was.[1]

Unrealized human potential is truly a sad reality on an individual basis. The tragedy is magnified when it occurs on a societal level.

Jason, a forensic investigator, shares how the nature of his work reveals a society in many ways "dying from within." He is called to go to wherever a death has occurred outside of a hospital or hospice. He has seen individuals as young as twelve take their life by suicide, and has read the notes they left behind. He has had to deal with some who have availed themselves of physician-assisted death, and has read those certificates as well. He is all too familiar with the havoc wrought by addiction, especially the newer drugs such as fentanyl that spare no one and often claim the unknowing and careless. Actually, he claims the street person is more likely to get life-saving help than many who appear to be affluent and die alone in isolation, without their cry for help being heard.

Rampant sexual abuse in and out of the Church, failed relationships, homelessness, human trafficking, greed and corruption, lust for power and control – all belie a society in desperate need of help, yet caught in the deadly web of denial. This is only touching the surface of this tragic iceberg, and is the opposite of what our destiny truly is.

Realizing Our Potential: An Invitation

Our Eastern cousins in the faith have been truer to the goal of realizing our full human potential than we in the West, with their focus on *theosis* or divinization/transformation as our final destiny. This is a goal we have largely sacrificed to technological progress, materialism and consumerism.

The Transfiguration of Jesus is a biblical account of precisely this reality: Jesus "was transfigured before them, and his face shone like the sun, and his clothes became dazzling white" (Matthew 17:2). Although the main purpose of this event was to offer the apostles courage to endure and have some understanding of the suffering Jesus would undergo in Jerusalem (in Luke 9:31, Moses and Elijah were speaking with Jesus "about his departure, which he was about to accomplish in Jerusalem"), it also reveals the glory that is ours, when "we will see face to face" (1 Corinthians 13:12).

Richard Rohr, in his online meditations, shares:

> As a young friar, I remember being very confused about Jesus beginning his preaching with the word 'change' (Mark 1:15, Matthew 3:2). What was I supposed to change from? I was a good Catholic, a Franciscan, soon to be a priest, and trying to keep my vows. I assumed he meant it for other 'bad' people. But those roles and identities were still all 'forms,' not necessarily the substance of my soul. I hope you get the point. The false self is all the more delusional the more it appears to be 'good.'[2]

This book seeks to sort out some of this confusion, explore the many dimensions of the elusive invitation to be fully human, realize our potential over a lifetime and welcome the second half of life, which is meant to be more reflective than the first. While gaining knowledge and accumulating experiences typifies the first half, I believe distilling wisdom out of that knowledge and experience characterizes the second half of life. Hopefully, the reflections shared in this book will help us move closer to the deepest yearnings of our heart, and experience greater serenity, joy, contentment and creativity in our lives. In the gospels, Jesus expresses this goal in one sentence: "I came that they may have life, and have it abundantly" (John 10:10).

This introduction began with the story of a boy wanting his newborn sibling to remind him of what God was like, for he was beginning to forget. A friend and soulmate prompted further reflection on this story. The need to change is inevitable if we truly want to grow, broaden our outlook on life, deepen our intellectual understanding and especially become more mature in our spirituality and our faith. But in our process of letting change take place, we still have to hold on to the one thing that is so important, that gives us meaning and our identity in God – our True Self. That young brother, caught up with the changes in his life, sensed he was losing the innocent, primal relationship with and knowledge of God that gave meaning to his existence in the first place, before his surroundings made their mark on him. And so, he turned to his new sibling for a reminder.

There is something here to which Rolheiser alludes in his writing about being tenderly caressed and kissed by God before we were born, a touch that left an imprint on the deepest part of our soul. That touch implanted in us a holy longing for the experience of the same love and tenderness that we strive to recover for the rest of our lives. Rohr would say we cannot yearn for something unless we have previously glimpsed it. Perhaps the ground of our being, which is uniquely "us" in God, is the source of this yearning, this need to continuously grow, heal and be transformed.

Given the nature of this book, I would suggest you read it with a trusted friend. I would also encourage you to write in the margins to express what is stirring within, and to keep a reflective journal to share with that friend who can offer additional insights and another perspective as you set out on this journey of being still green and growing.

There is a saying that "When a drop of water falls into the ocean, the ocean is changed." If this book can be that drop of water making a difference in even one person's life, offering them hope and empowering them to experience even a little growth and transformation, then it will be more than worth the penning of it.

1

Incarnational Spirituality: The Art of Being Human

God accepts us as we are,
and believes in whom we can become.

—*Sr. Teresita Kambeitz OSU*

That one sentence from Sr. Teresita Kambeitz OSU, educator and former superior general of the Ursulines of Prelate, summarizes this book. We will study more deeply who we are as human beings on this planet and explore who it is our loving Creator God is inviting us to become, especially in our sunset years.

For some mysterious reason, from deep within and for all these years of life and ministry, the need to be fully human has served as a starting point for much of my ministry. Part of this may come from my personal make-up, nature and background, but also from the many influences in my life over the years.

Walking the Way Jesus Walked

The first major influence has to be that of the master himself. From his conception in Mary's womb, his birth or Incarnation (the Word was made flesh), his humble life among us, his passion, death and resurrection, and his appearances to his friends, Jesus was first and foremost fully and totally human. He never once fell for the temptation to use his divinity in a selfish way.

This is clearly established at the beginning of his ministry in the gospels, especially in the episode on the temptations. That incident begins with another very deliberately chosen fully human event – his baptism in the Jordan. Even John the Baptist, who proclaimed him as the Lamb of God, protested that Jesus should have baptized him, but Jesus gently insisted, "it is proper for us in this way to fulfill all righteousness" (Matthew 3:15). This "righteousness" was Jesus' commitment to be totally faithful to the Father and obey the humble and unexpected way God's plan to reveal the depth of God's love for the world and to the world would be played out. The Father's blessing, "This is my Son, the beloved, with whom I am well pleased," grounded Jesus in the Father's love, filled him with "human security," and empowered him to be totally obedient to his mission.

According to the gospel of Mark, the Spirit immediately drove Jesus out into the wilderness after he was blessed by the Father to be tempted by Satan (Mark 1:12-13). Mark places an emphasis on "drove out" because as the New Israel, Jesus had to be tempted in every way the Chosen People of God were tempted in the wilderness. Those temptations were to become overly attached to land, status and independence, to the point that these became false gods. In the recovery program of Alcoholics Anonymous, these are spoken of simply as money, fame and power. I prefer to enumerate them as the abuse of possessions and pleasure, prestige and fame, power and control. Jesus would prove to be totally faithful to the Father and reject all those temptations to which the Israelites consistently and stubbornly succumbed.

With imagination, one can explore what happened in this encounter between Jesus and Satan (Matthew 4:1-11). Satan first approached Jesus and mocked him, saying, in effect, "How can you be the Son of God you claim to be if you are so poor? Turn these stones into bread. Put your faith and trust in possessions and pleasure. That is what will make you happy." Jesus, so secure in the Father's love for him, replied that he did not need to be rich to be the Son of God: "One does not live by bread alone, but by every word that comes from the mouth of God."

So, Satan tried a second time. He took Jesus to a pinnacle on top of the temple and asked him to throw himself down to make the angels come and save him. Satan was saying, "How can you be the Son of God when you are a big fat nobody? You're not famous – no one knows anything about you." Jesus, so secure in the Father's love for him, replied that he did not need fame or prestige to be the Son of God: "Do not put the Lord your God to the test." He would take the steps down like everybody else.

Twice rebuffed, Satan tempted Jesus a third and final time, taking him up a high mountain where he showed and promised Jesus all the kingdoms of the world if Jesus would only fall down and worship him. Satan was saying to Jesus, "How can you be the Son of God if you have no power or control over anybody or anything?" Jesus, again so secure in the Father's love for him, answered that he did not need to have power or control to be the Son of God: "Away with you, Satan! For it is written, 'Worship the Lord your God, and serve only him.'" Then the devil left him until an opportune time, when Jesus would be most vulnerable – on the cross. He would be tempted to come down from the cross, to avoid suffering and dying, to be unfaithful to his Father and to his commitment to be both fully human and reveal to us the depth of the Father's love.

This humble humanity of Jesus, this way of being totally faithful to the Father, from crib to cross, is a profound mystery and challenge that goes against almost every grain of our being. We struggle with this challenge every day, which may explain why it seems so easy for even church members and pastoral folks to give it lip service and justify an un-Jesus-like attraction to money, fame and power as being simply practical and necessary. This is why it needs to be put forward, talked about, espoused and lived much more closely in everything we do – to strive to walk as Jesus walked (1 John 2:6).

Other Major Influences

There are many who have walked as Jesus walked, who have influenced this focus on Incarnational spirituality. One is the first-century bishop-martyr St. Irenaeus of Antioch, who taught the glory of God is men and women fully alive.[3] In that light, all we need to do as human beings is be the best person we can be and live life to the full.

Recently, some friends asked me what I thought of the re-mark Pope Francis often makes: that he is a sinner. While I can understand his motive for the comment – to avoid being put on a pedestal because of his office – I appreciated their critique that such a statement runs the risk of defining the essence of who we are as sinful, rather than as a beloved child of God who sometimes fails and sins – a big distinction. Even the comment "I am only human," sometimes used to excuse oneself from some sinful behaviour, is flawed in their view, because it denigrates our humanity. The more I thought about this perspective, the more I realized that both these statements about being a sinner and being only human also take something away from that declara-tion of St. Irenaeus – God's glory is displayed when we live fully our humanity. This view deepened my stance on Incarnational spirituality, and for that I am grateful.

Another mentor in my life has been Jean Vanier, son of the former governor-general of Canada. As founder of L'Arche, a movement providing a family-style community life for the people with developmental disabilities, he has learned much from these people who are so often isolated and excluded. One of the lessons he learned is this:

> To be human is to accept who we are, this mixture of strength and weakness. To be human is to accept and love others just as they are. To be human is to be bonded together, each with our weaknesses and strengths, because we need each other. Weakness, recognized, accepted and offered is at the heart of belonging, so it is at the heart of communion with another.[4]

When I heard Vanier speak years ago, I gained a key insight into being human that has shaped my approach to life ever since: "When we are humble, open and honest enough to share our weakness with our brothers and sisters, that frees them to be humble, open and honest enough to share their weakness with us, and together we grow." It is our weakness and brokenness, not our strength and perfection, that serve as a catalyst for growth and healing.

Recent years have been difficult ones for the Church, which has gone through its share of crisis and scandals, many of them having to do with finances, human sexuality and the Indian residential school legacy in Canada. Archbishop Anthony Mancini is one who inherited a sexual abuse scandal in his archdiocese. I admired how he handled this crisis with courage, compassion and a profound desire to help us all understand the nature of that reality. Here is an excerpt from a pastoral letter he wrote in response to the crisis:

> If our church is to get beyond our present difficulties, if we hope to have any significant future, we must learn the lessons which these last years of struggle point to. One of these lessons is for all of us to have a better understanding of what constitutes a human person. People, priests and bishops are human, and failure to see, recognize and care about this will continue to produce inhuman expectations and give rise to inhuman behavior.

This call to have a better understanding of the human person is an underlying theme of this book, and one reason why this first chapter is dedicated to precisely that goal.

As a new coadjutor archbishop, I had the opportunity to meet now emeritus Pope Benedict during the Ad Limina visit of the Western bishops to Rome in 2006. We talked about his first encyclical, *Deus Caritas Est* (God is Love), in which he addresses love from a Christian perspective and God's place within all love. Impressed by that document, I wasn't surprised to see in his third encyclical, *Caritas In Veritate* (Charity in Truth), his emphasis on two truths Pope Paul VI proclaimed in his encyclical *Populorum Progressio*: "The whole Church, in all her being and acting – when she proclaims, when she celebrates, when she performs works of charity – is engaged in promoting integral human development," and "Authentic human development concerns the whole of the person in every single dimension."[5]

Those comments from Paul VI, highlighted by Benedict XVI, affirmed my own emphasis on personal growth and being human. Spiritual writer Dom Basil Pennington OCSO adds this gentle, supportive reflection that I have summarized as follows:

Parents often invest too much of themselves in the success of their children. Feeling they will be judged a success or a failure, they begin to trade off on their love for the child to get the child to perform in a certain way or they will not be loved. The message this gives to the little ones is they are not loveable in themselves. Their value depends on what they have, what they do, what others – especially significant providers, real or potential – think of them. This is the construct of the false self. It is made up of what I have, what I do and what others think of me.[6]

The simple way Pennington writes can almost prevent us from appreciating the sublime wisdom garnered from a lifetime of pastoral practice and reflection.

Our True and False Selves

These comments lead us into reflecting on our true and false selves as an integral part of our humanity. One who writes extensively on this topic is Rohr, as in this sampling from his book *Immortal Diamond*:

Both True Self and False Self will feel like your "self," so you see the confusion … We might now call the False Self our small self or ego, and we might call the True Self our soul … Your soul is who you are in God and who God is in you … Our True Self knows there is no place to go or to get to. We are already home – free and filled. That is the essence of the good news … This is your soul. It is God-in-you. This is your True Self.[7]

Elsewhere, Rohr writes,

Like used scaffolding, our sins fall away from us as un-needed and unhelpful because now a new and better building has been found. This is the wondrous discovery of our True Self, and the gradual deterioration of our false and constructed self.[8]

While Rohr's writings cover a broad spectrum of issues and topics, his thoughts, insights and reflections on our true and false selves and the two halves of life are especially valuable for the purpose of this book, so I will lean extensively on him.

James Martin SJ, another prolific author, well-known speaker and student of Thomas Merton, notes that Merton

> often distinguished between the 'false self' and the 'true self.' The false self is the person we present to the world, the one we think will be pleasing to others: attractive, confident and successful. The true self, on the other hand, is the person we are before God. Sanctity consists in discovering who that person is and striving to become that person. As Merton wrote, 'For me to be a saint means to be myself.'[9]

I find it remarkable that Merton, a Trappist monk, would write so succinctly on the human person. Remarkable, but not surprising, as he did not become a monk to escape the world, but to hold in his heart the suffering of the world. This stance certainly allowed him to develop his thoughts on what it means to be human.

Rolheiser offers some theological insights into our "best or true" self, based on the word "repent." Unfortunately, the English word "repent" does not convey the profound meaning of the word that in Greek is rendered *metanoia*. *Meta* means "highest or biggest," like metaphysics. *Noia* derives from the Greek *nous*, which means "mind." The term *metanoia* thus has the sense of "putting on our highest mind," of being our best self.

The image of our true self is an open palm, as the late spiritual writer Henri Nouwen describes it so well in his book *With Open Hands*; although dated, it is well worth reading. The opposite of *metanoia* is *paranoia*, or being "beside oneself." The image of our false self is a closed fist: it involves being closed in, protective, wearing masks and living in denial, impeding any personal growth at all.

An Indigenous legend offers us a pertinent insight: A troubled young boy approached an elder with a personal dilemma. He felt there was a struggle within him between an attraction to the good and a constant tug to the bad that he likened to two wolves fighting within him. The young lad wondered which one would win, to which the elder replied, "The one you feed."

Similarly, we have within us two minds: a higher mind linked to our best self, and a lower mind linked to our baser self. Which one is us? Both of them are. As Rolheiser puts it, some days we are like Mother Teresa and can walk on water, and other days, we are easily annoyed, impatient and not that likeable. It all depends on which mind we are operating out of. Our task is to repent, do *metanoia* and try to live out of our highest mind as our way of being and living.

I would add the following:

Our True Self is not only the self that operates out of our higher mind, but also the self that is open to newness, to the "more" life has to offer, to help from others along the way. It is the self with humility to see ourselves as we are, and especially the ability to be mentally true to ourselves and speak our truth.

The Medicine Wheel

Years of ministry among the Indigenous peoples of Western Canada have led me to greatly appreciate the Medicine Wheel as a model for walking in harmony and living a balanced, full human life. A basic version of the wheel (physical, mental, emotional and spiritual) invites us to take care of ourselves physically, to pursue a lifetime of learning and reflecting, to be aware of and deal with our emotions, and to develop a mature, intimate relationship with God in prayer.

The Medicine Wheel has an interesting contrast with the three-step method Cardinal Joseph Cardijn taught the Church in the early 1960s: See, Judge, Act. Pope John XXIII recognized this method in his May 1961 encyclical *Mater et Magistra*; it was later adopted by proponents of liberation theology as a tool for social analysis. The Medicine Wheel adds "feeling" to seeing, judging and acting, thus completing the Cardijn model by honouring and taking into consideration the emotional dimension.

We proceed around the Medicine Wheel as follows:

* In the direction of the East, we mindfully take in with our senses a great deal of information.
* In the direction of the South, we process this information intellectually, forming the basis of our belief system.
* Our belief system, positive or warped, influences the way we feel, in the direction of the West.
* This emotional energy influences our behaviour in the direction of the North. All too often, we act out of our emotions in destructive ways if we don't deal with them positively.

Emotional Intelligence

The area of our emotions is where we, for some reason, struggle the most, yet they are integral to the Medicine Wheel and to living in balance. Emotions are powerful energy that must go somewhere. They deal with us if we don't deal with them. We transmit the pain we don't transform through horizontal or lateral violence. To deny or suppress our emotions is to emotionally abuse ourselves, resist our God who created us to feel, and break the commandment to love ourselves. The Marriage Encounter movement teaches that emotions have no morality: they are neither right nor wrong. They just are. This in itself is a liberating truth. The best thing we can do with painful emotions is share them – they lose their power over us when shared.

I believe all emotions are positive, no matter how painful. There is no such thing as a negative emotion – all are a gift from God carrying a message from our inner child to our True Self. They are letting us know who we are at that moment and in those circumstances.

The art of living life to the full leads us into a holistic manner of living, respecting and honouring all these dimensions of being truly and fully human. It invites us to walk in balance, harmony, purpose and serenity, and finds its roots in faith, to which we turn our attention now.

2

Rooted in Faith, Growing in Hope, Living in Love

Faith is how you know where you are going.
Hope is what keeps you going.
Love is how you get there.

—Author unknown

A Life-giving Pattern

A scene in the 1989 movie *Indiana Jones and the Last Crusade* was like a punch in the stomach for me. At one point, the hero climbs a high mountain and comes to a deep chasm he must cross – on faith. After some hesitation, he steps out into the abyss, and instantly an invisible bridge shoots across to support him.

One could say it is only a movie, but that scene seared itself into my mind, heart and even soul as a dramatic image of what deep, profound faith in God's providence looks like. At the same time, I knew my faith was nowhere near this level. This painful feeling was mitigated somewhat by the fact that I knew we can always grow in faith, hope and love.

There is a faith pattern in our lives: faith in God's love for us leads to the hope of life always getting better and the possibility of change and growth. In turn, a vibrant hope empowers us to give our lives away in love. The opposite pattern is doubt, despair and death.

> The opposite of love isn't really hate, but death – without love, we wither and die.

An Infinite Horizon

Pierre Olivier Tremblay, an Oblate who ministered to university students and was recently named bishop, believes the youth he encountered on a daily basis lack hope. The reason they lack hope is they do not have a bigger picture, a larger story, a meta-narrative, an infinite horizon provided by faith into which they can place the events of their lives. All they are left with is what happens to them on a particular day. If this is a painful reality such as the break-up of a relationship, they have no faith buffer, nothing with which to soften the blow. Some even end up taking their lives in despair.

In its own simple way, an old catechism gave children (and adults, too) that infinite horizon and meta-narrative with the question "Why did God make us?" and the straightforward answer "To know, love and serve God in this life, and to be eternally happy with him in the next."

There it is – a bigger picture, a meta-narrative, an infinite horizon into which we can place and handle the more painful events of our lives. Like the woman who wanted to be buried with a fork in her hand because her mother always told her, "Keep your fork – the best is yet to come," we know there is more to life than just what we experience. Some of our parents grew up with the prayer/hymn "Hail, Holy Queen," which on the surface seems negative, but carries within it the infinite horizon allowing them to accept hardships and disappointments without succumbing to them. Here are some of the lines:

> To thee do we cry, poor banished children of Eve.
> To thee do we send up our sighs,
> mourning and weeping in this valley of tears.

Faith allows us to accept that this life is sometimes a valley of tears, and this is okay, because we know that is not all there is to life – there is much more. Eternal life will more than make up for the shortcomings of this life. In its own way, the country song "I Never Promised You a Rose Garden" imparts the same message. The youth of today seem to no longer know this final ending of our human story!

Secure in Love

A biblical event that strikingly and almost shockingly conveys the blessings of having a strong faith and meta-narrative is the washing of feet in the gospel of John (John 13:1-15). Jesus, so secure in the Father's love for him – and knowing he came from the Father, all things had been given to him by the Father, and he was returning to the Father – was able to take off his outer robes symbolizing power, control, authority, position, status and prestige, and wash the feet of his disciples, the task of a slave. Jesus then challenged his disciples (and us) to do the same, something that only being rooted in faith, hope and love can empower us to do. Being secure in the Father's love for us makes it possible to wash others' feet through both dialogue with those whose views differ from ours and attempts at reconciliation whenever a relationship has been weakened or broken.

Contemplative Prayer

The blessing Jesus received from the Father at his baptism grounded him in the Father's love for him, a rootedness strengthened by his intimate prayerful relationship with the Father. The gospels mention he would often slip away and spend the whole night in prayer, communing with the Father and soaking up the Father's love (Luke 6:12). If Jesus felt the need to do this, should we not do the same?

One of the best ways for us to commune with our loving God is by means of contemplative prayer. This kind of prayer differs from discursive prayer, in which we talk to God. In contemplative prayer, God does the talking and we do the listening, or perhaps more accurately, God acts and we are just present. It is important to remember, as the late Trappist monk and spiritual writer Thomas Keating often points out, "God's first language is silence."[10] So, we have to enter into "sheer silence" to really hear what God is communicating to us, like Elijah did in his cave (1 Kings 19:12).

In contemplative prayer, we are simply in God's presence, trying not to think or feel anything. It is a powerful act of faith – trusting that in the silence, God is doing whatever God wants to do within us, healing and transforming us at a subconscious level. As the letter to the Hebrews puts it, "Indeed, the word of God is living and active, sharper than any two-edged sword, piercing until it divides soul from spirit, joints from marrow; it is able to judge the thoughts and intentions of the heart" (4:12).

At its deepest level, contemplative prayer is a free choice to place ourselves into the space of radical discipleship and the Dark Night of the Spirit[11] that, barring an accident that cuts our life short, will come to us by conscription when we are in a seniors' home. Those stages of our lives, which we will discuss later in this book, are designed by nature to lead us into doing the inner work and purification preparing us for death. We freely choose to waste time – so as to make the most of our time here on earth – by placing ourselves into "spiritual palliative care"! This is an important component of contemplative prayer.

Lectio Divina

Virginia called me one day, complaining she could no longer pray. It no longer appealed to her, and she had lost her desire to pray all those prayers she was accustomed to praying. Her sharing surprised me, because she was such a faithful person, had taken the Christopher Leadership Course, was involved with her family in Search weekend retreats, was a reader in her parish and had been Rectora for a Cursillo weekend.

I thought of St. Paul, who at one point told the Corinthians they had been feeding on spiritual milk, and now he wanted to give them spiritual solid food by which they could be nourished (1 Corinthians 3:2-3). With this in mind, I suggested her problem was not being unable to pray; it was a case of her being ready for a more mature kind of prayer. I introduced her to Lectio Divina and she was off and running with a new eagerness to pray.

Lectio Divina is an ancient method of contemplative prayer that is being rediscovered today. It moves us from discursive to contemplative prayer. In its simplest form, it consists of four distinct stages:

1. *Lectio* (reading) – we prayerfully read a passage of scripture;

2. *Meditatio* (meditation) – we ponder the passage, asking ourselves what God is saying to us through it at this time of our lives. We may also read a commentary on the passage;

3. *Oratio* (prayer) – we pray with the words of the passage for the needs of the world and our own intentions; and finally

4. *Contemplatio* (contemplation) – here we just rest in the presence of God, trying not to feel or think anything. If a brilliant insight or powerful emotion comes to us, we don't cling to it. We just acknowledge it, thank God for it, place it in an imaginary canoe and let it slip away. In contemplation we allow God to do whatever God wants to do within us, believing that the Spirit of God, through a kind of divine therapy, is healing us deep within.[12]

Some would add a fifth stage, *Operatio* (action), which consists of finding some way to apply our prayer experience to our daily lives. Most often, *Operatio* becomes for me writing a homily for the day or for the coming Sunday, and then trying to live what I have written. Influenced by Marriage Encounter, I also write a love letter to Jesus, sharing with him my feelings about the word with which I have prayed during my holy hour.

That love letter is an excellent way to foster a more intimate relationship with Jesus, as it did with my father when I wrote him a letter eleven years after he died sharing all my feelings about the way he raised us. Reading that letter out loud to him transformed our relationship – I was no longer a child and he a big daddy; it was more like an adult-to-adult relationship now. We were friends because we had shared feelings. That is also when I believe I received the spirit of my father to be with me in a new way. That was an amazing experience of the Communion of Saints, as I had the distinct feeling I was helping my father enter heaven. One can't put a price tag on spiritual realities like that.

A biblical model for this kind of prayer is Mary of Bethany, who, according to Keating, was sitting at the feet of Jesus (the posture of a disciple) not so much listening to his words, but rather aware that she was in the presence of *the* Word, and that was enough – just soaking up Jesus' love (Luke 10:38-42). Can we try to be like Mary and soak up God's love more often?

I witnessed an image of soaking up God's love while visiting a friend. His fifteen-year-old daughter returned from a soccer tournament, barged into the house, threw down her duffel bag, made a beeline to her father, sat on his lap, put her arm around his neck and leaned her head against his, silently soaking up her father's love. He calmly kept on talking to me over her, while his wife continued preparing supper and her siblings carried on playing.

I was deeply moved by the wordless, intimate relationship between a father and daughter, and felt warm all over as I drove away. It struck me this was as close as I would ever get to seeing God with my eyes in this life. This was also an image of contemplative prayer. The daughter never said a word to her father – she just soaked up his love. This is contemplative prayer at its best – soaking up the Father's love, like John resting his head on Jesus' chest at the Last Supper, listening to his heart beat (John 13:23).

Praying as an Anawim

Another manner of praying I have found indispensable to my own personal growth and healing is praying as an *Anawim*. This Hebrew word refers to the poor people who know they need God, who have no pretensions, no ego getting in the way, no masks to hide behind, or sophistication that blurs or buries reality.

I learned this kind of prayer the hard way as a young missionary priest in my first mission. Suddenly put in charge by an unforeseen development, I reacted by hitting the road running. Unaware that I was a workaholic and had a messiah complex, a Mr.

Fix-It way of being, and a naïve attitude of superiority, I set about working day and night, thinking I could solve everyone's problems in no time. However, by the end of that first year, I was exhausted, frustrated, and on the verge of burnout. I felt like quitting the priesthood. Someone shared with me their observation that I had been there for a year already and nothing had changed. I felt very angry at that person, hurt and confused – what was wrong?

Then I was unexpectedly given a small pamphlet by Stuart Briscoe entitled "This is Exciting." That I still remember the author and title reveals how significant this incident was for me at the time. In it I read how he found Christianity easy for the first 20 years of his life, then found it hard after he went to the seminary and tried to be perfect (I could identify immediately). Then he realized it was neither easy nor hard, which left me puzzled until I turned the page and read... it was impossible.

Suddenly, I understood the problem – I was trying to do the impossible! I was doing my will in God's name, which T.S. Eliot described in the drama *Murder in the Cathedral* with these words: "To do the right thing for the wrong reason is the greatest kind of treason." I went jogging in the northern jack pine forest, stood before a pine tree, and surrendered my will to God. I accepted that these were his people, not mine; this was his church, not mine. A huge load was lifted off my shoulders, joy and lightness filled my heart, and I was healed!

I felt affirmed when I realized this is the prayer St. Peter learned walking on the water (Matthew 14:28-32). His first prayer, "Lord, command me to come to you," was from his head and somewhat prideful. Then, because I am so much like Peter, I can guess what happened next. He was walking on water – which was amazing – took his eyes off Jesus, looked back at the boat to show off what he was doing, felt the wind and started to sink. He was drowning; his prayer changed to three words from his gut: "Lord, save me!" Immediately, Jesus was there to pick him up by the shoulder and ask, "You of little faith, why did you doubt?"

What do you think Peter did next – let go and try on his own again, or hang on to Jesus and walk together with him back to the boat? I am certain he did the latter, and so must we.

> I now believe it is impossible for us to live even one day the way Jesus wants us to, joyous and free, without his help. Anyone can get through a given day if they are stubborn or scared enough, but they will do so with no personal change or inner healing happening.

To pray as an *Anawim* is to utter a humble prayer from the heart acknowledging our need and asking for help. So, every morning since that liberating experience described above, the first thing I do upon rising is get on my knees and ask for the help of the Spirit of the Risen Lord, just for that day, one day at a time. This prayer eventually became an appendix entitled "Twelve by Twenty-four" in my book *Walk a New Path*, on addictions awareness. As step eleven of the Twelve Step program states, "We sought to improve our conscious contact with God" – and that is what praying as an *Anawim* is all about. It has made a difference for over forty years in my life, and I would encourage you to try it.

Blessed and Blessing

Authors who write on male spirituality speak of the importance of blessing and being blessed. A key role of an elder is to bless the youth they encounter along life's way. To bless is to let go of one's ego, to step aside, to make room for a younger person, to refrain from competing with that person, to put that younger person's future above one's own, and to accept, perhaps with some grieving, that one has passed one's prime.

A good example of a blessing is Jean Val Jean in the movie *Les Misérables*. At one point, he goes to the barricade to find the young man who is in love with his adopted daughter, and who will ultimately take her away from him. Instead of resisting this flow of life, he prays as an elder, a king, and asks God to bless the young man, keep him safe and, if need be, take his own life instead of the young man's. He puts the young man's well-being and future over and above his own.

To bless comes from the Latin *benedicere*, which means "to speak well of." To bless, then, is to encourage, build up, affirm, strengthen and empower others to be more generative in whatever their walk of life might be. Something happens, something shifts within, when one is blessed by an elder.

I must admit I had taken all this teaching on the importance of blessing rather lightly until I had an experience of being blessed by an elder during a retreat I gave for a group of my fellow Oblates. When I learned that Archbishop emeritus Adam Exner OMI was to attend the retreat, I was surprised and intimidated. Exner was my spiritual director and professor. At age ninety-three, he was going to take this somewhat unusual retreat dealing with addictions awareness and the Twelve Step program, addressing issues such as forgiveness, grieving, healing and, of all things, even touching on human sexuality! How would he accept all this? I wondered.

During my presentations, I was surprised at how many times I referred to something Exner had taught me over the years: my need to work on my relationship with my father, getting in touch with God's unconditional love for me through Isaiah 43:1-4; my need to fail miserably at something and still be accepted by the people in my first mission, praying as an *Anawim*, lowering my expectations, taking a thirty-day retreat before my ordination to the priesthood, and being a disciple, to name a few things, means becoming a carbon copy of Jesus.

What really got to me, however, was his comment in the thank-you card given to me at the end: "The student has surpassed the teacher – I'm proud of you."

I was stopped in my tracks, shocked, stunned, speechless, almost disbelieving. But there it was: "The student has surpassed the teacher – I'm proud of you." Then other feelings flooded in like a tsunami. I felt uplifted, energized, empowered, appreciated, loved, transported to a higher level … in the end, blessed! It was so true – what Rolheiser and Rohr have been teaching all along, the need to bless and be blessed – and now I felt the power of that blessing.

Exner, for me at that moment, was truly an elder, a wise old man, a king, an older bishop who could humbly step aside, bless a younger bishop, and help that younger bishop be more generative. I felt grateful beyond words, and inspired to do likewise – to bless, empower, affirm others, help them be generative, and in that humble stance, find pure joy. What a model he is for me, for us all, and an inspiration to become an elder like him as we age – able to bless and give life to those who are younger.

When Rolheiser speaks of the power of blessing, he often quotes the following poem by William Butler Yeats:

My fiftieth year come and gone.
I sit, a solitary man,
In a crowded London shop,
An open book and empty cup
On a marble table-top.

While on the shop and street I gazed
My body of a sudden blazed;
And twenty minutes more or less
It seemed so great my happiness
That I was blessed and could bless.[13]

Once a month, I go to a remand centre to celebrate the Eucharist with a pod of inmates who are waiting for their fate to be made known. One group of seventeen women, all in yellow prison garb, touched my heart during a celebration in their obvious need for affirmation and love. I was inspired to ritually facilitate some love for them. First, I had them give themselves a hug "because they deserved it." Then I went around the circle, looking them in the eye, placing a hand on a shoulder, and declaring to each one sincerely, "You are a beloved daughter of God." They could respond as they wished to these words. I invited them to follow me in a give-and-receive ritual. They were on a natural high after that experience of both blessing and being blessed, of loving each other and of being loved.

If our faith, hope and love can move us more and more into that stance of seeing with blessed eyes our own beauty, and the beauty of others and our world, especially as elders, then this world will truly be a better place for our being in it.

3

Spirituality as a Transformative Power

God comes to us disguised as our life.

—*Paula D'Arcy*

The spiritual life has much more to do with subtraction than it does with addition.

—*Meister Eckhart*

There is a crack in everything. That's how the light gets in.

—*Leonard Cohen*[14]

The Role of Spirituality

René Fumoleau, a veteran Oblate missionary in the Northwest Territories, has an interesting way of viewing the relationship between faith and spirituality. He sees spirituality as being an underground stream, and all the different denominations as wells drilling down to tap into that underground stream of living water.

Much has been written about spirituality. For the purpose of this book, I will distill only some pertinent definitions. A main one would be that spirituality is all about relationship and connectedness. One of our most basic human needs is to belong to others and, more basically, to our God, who is our life force. We are created to relate, to be in relationship, and therein lies both our greatest joy and our greatest struggle. As human beings, we yearn for intimacy, yet live in fear of it, for it would open us up to being hurt. Nevertheless, that need to be connected remains powerful, and led St. Augustine to articulate his famous saying: "You have made us for yourself, O Lord, and our heart is restless until it rests in you."[15]

Of the many other things written about spirituality, another stands out: spirituality is all about transformation.

With movies and books like *The Shack* and *The Divine Dance* that present a dynamic, relational, fluid, interpersonal image of God as a continuous flow of love and energy among three persons, Father, Son and Holy Spirit, this view of spirituality makes more and more sense. To be connected with this dynamic source of relational energy is to be caught up in an eternal *perichoresis*, or divine dance,[16] that is always moving, growing, becoming, and beckoning us to be more and more transformed into that image and likeness.

St. Paul expresses this well in his reminder to the Corinthians (and us as well) of their destiny: "Now the Lord is the Spirit, and where the Spirit of the Lord is, there is freedom. And all of us, with unveiled faces, seeing the glory of the Lord as though reflected in a mirror, are being transformed into the same image from one degree of glory to another; for this comes from the Lord, the Spirit" (2 Corinthians 3:17-18).

This passage leapt out at me during a private retreat some years ago. Perhaps the saying "When the student is ready, the teacher will appear" holds true here. It has served as an undergirding for much of my prayer and reflection ever since. It is obvious in this passage that St. Paul has caught not only the final goal of a dynamic faith, but also the insight that being a faith-filled human in all its dimensions involves a constant process of change, healing, growth and transformation. I cannot think of a better way to articulate spirituality as transformation, although Richard Rohr comes close with this thought in his online meditation on Interfaith Friendship: "In the end, all spirituality really is about transformation, dying before we die and being reborn as our True Selves in love."[17]

Appreciating Our Human Sexuality

Taking more seriously this area of human sexuality, which has been neglected for far too long in the Church, can help us live well and age graciously.

Thankfully, there is a revival of this spirituality recently, beginning with writers such as Robert Bly and Joseph Campbell, and continued especially by Rohr, to whom again I am indebted for much of the following material.

Rohr has a vision to change the world in five years, beginning with men. He sees fourteen-year-old boys in developing countries who own little more than a loincloth walking around their community like men because they have been initiated and blessed by their elders: they feel they belong and know how to be men. He returns to North America to find thirty-year-old men driving sports cars and acting like boys because they have never been initiated or blessed by their elders, don't know how to be men and are self-initiating in high-risk ways: driving too fast, drinking too much, having sex too soon. They are destroying themselves.

Rohr's response to this scenario is to create a critical mass of initiated men who will help initiate young boys into manhood, through the Illuman organization including MALES (Men as Leaders and Elders) and events such as Men's Rites of Passage (MROP), a movement that is now spreading around the world.

Whenever one deals with gender issues, it can be a minefield of misunderstanding, stirred-up emotions and demands for political correctness. Nevertheless, I think it needs to be stated that from time immemorial, every culture in the world has male and female archetypal energy forms: warrior, lover, magus and King for men; maiden, mother and Crone (or Sophia) for women. "Crone" is an old English word with both negative and positive connotations. Fortunately, women today are reclaiming this term and embracing its values, which appreciate older women for their judgment, experience, wisdom (Sophia) and being in a position to influence others. The remainder of this book will use the term "Sophia."

In today's world, these archetypes can be critiqued as an outdated and somewhat sexist anthropology. Just how this anthropology fits in with today's emphasis on non-dualistic thinking and non-binary terminology is up for debate, but that is beyond the scope of this book, which is seeking to explore the traditional male-female journey.

That being said, traditionally boys are born to be warriors with phallic energy who naturally strive to get to the top, to compete, to tussle, to outdo one another. To stay on the warrior journey too long, however, is to risk becoming a bitter old fool, because there is more to life than fighting and getting to the top. Rohr posits three choices: become a pathetic old fool (trying to stay young by every means possible), a bitter old fool (unable to let go of the need to compete and be at the top) or a wise old fool (a serene king or elder).

To become wise old fools, boys have to be knocked off the warrior path, descend, learn to relate more deeply, pray more profoundly and finally become kings, elders, wise older men. Initiation rites involving some suffering and shedding of blood are designed to provide that service to young boys, who must learn the lessons of initiation: "Life is hard. You are not that important. Your life is not about you. You are not in control. You are going die."[18]

Girls, on the other hand, start out life as maidens. They shed blood through menstruation and suffer the pain of childbirth as they become mothers. Older women need to ascend, to assert themselves, because they innately know the wisdom flowing from their experience, to become Sophia, elders, wise old women. To not ascend puts them at risk of becoming angry old women, although the more common term is "witch on a broom." Women know about shedding blood and suffering, so they don't need initiation rites. Young girls need coming-of-age rites celebrating their power to give life and teaching them how to be women.

Sadly, we have lost this powerful cultural and spiritual source of growth and maturation in our sophisticated Western society, and we are paying the price. I know of only one family that had an initiation rite for their young son, and one family that had a coming-of-age rite for their daughter. In both cases, the youth were blessed and privileged to have had that experience. These rites are to help us descend or ascend on the path leading us to our goal of serving others as Kings or Sophia.

The ultimate goal is for King and Sophia to journey together as elders. An elder's deep and studied passion carries so much more power than superficial and loudly stated principles. I have had the joyful privilege of taking workshops given by Indigenous couples who certainly were a source of peace and healing for all the participants – taking turns presenting and sharing their wisdom and maturity. The latest experience for me was with elders A.J. and Patricia and their presentation at a workshop that will be discussed later.

I also personally experienced the power of male spirituality on a retreat at Ghost Ranch in New Mexico with Rohr many years ago. I had just come from a leadership discernment session of our Oblate province, during which my name had not even appeared on the board. Thinking I had lost the respect of my brother Oblates, I felt sad, overlooked, somewhat dejected on my arrival at the ranch. The first night of the retreat, Rohr explained the male journey. When he spoke about the bitter old fool, I suddenly realized he was talking about me! I was wanting to be back in leadership, on top again. As the talk went on, it dawned on me that I was the one who needed to descend, let go of wanting to be on top, move in the direction of deeper relationships and enter more deeply into contemplative prayer on my way to becoming an elder, a king, a wise old man. The pressure I was putting on myself disappeared and I was able to enter into that retreat with a whole new understanding and lighter spirit.

A Spirituality of Human Incompleteness

This view of spirituality, based largely on St. John of the Cross as interpreted by Rolheiser, remains for me one of the most comprehensive, insightful and beneficial views of the mystery of being human to date. As I wrote extensively about this in my previous book, *Walk a New Path*, I will just summarize it here.

The definition itself is this: "The tension of living positively our human incompleteness."

Standing alone, and at first glance, it probably says little to the casual reader. However, with the help of Indigenous spirituality in the form of the Medicine Wheel, it can take on profound and far-reaching proportions.

Within this definition, we will adapt the basic Medicine Wheel by inserting the word "relational" in the place of "spiritual," which we will set aside for now. As human beings, we relate to God, others, ourselves and all of God's creation. The centre of the wheel becomes human sexuality, or Eros.

Why would that be? one might ask. When we are born, what is the first question that is asked of us? The answer is one of gender – is it a boy or a girl? We are an "it" until that is verified. And that is a matter of human sexuality. The word "sex" comes from the Latin *secare*, meaning "cut off" or "separated from." A branch cut off from a tree is thus "sexed." Any farmer from Saskatchewan knows this instinctively, because much of the prairie land there is measured in sections, one mile by one mile, one section being 640 acres. That land is "sexed"!

Biblical theology now takes us deeper into this human reality. In Genesis, we hear God making this pronouncement: "Let us make humankind in our image, according to our likeness ... so God created humankind in his image ... male and female he created them" (Genesis 1:26-27). The key word is the plural "our". Why would God speak like that, especially in the Old Testament, before any hint of revelation of God as Trinity? The answer lies in royalty – the majestic plural. It is a king or queen, or perhaps the pope, who would speak like that: "We have decided …." So, we are born, male or female, with kingly and queenly, God-like energy. We are royalty!

That reality makes us very special, but it also poses a challenge. God can hold male and female energy together, but we cannot. We are born male or female, and thus incomplete. That creates a holy longing, a divine fire, an all-encompassing yearning for consummation and wholeness deep within us, an Eros, a sexual energy, that is constant and pervasive. That energy is what attracts male and female to each other like a powerful magnet. It is holy energy, an especially powerful energy meant to be used according to God's will and purpose, within a committed relationship and marriage.

That energy is a desire to see the face of God. Within the context of a committed relationship, it is holy. To take that energy out of the safe container of commitment, and to splash it on a screen or glossy paper, is to try to see the face of God the wrong way. That can and does become pornography that is too powerful for us and burns us, like grasping a high-powered electrical wire without protective coating. Because that addiction is so powerful, and today with the internet, so pervasive and destructive, we need to ponder it more closely.

When two persons in a committed relationship like marriage achieve intimacy that is physical, mental, emotional and relational, their bed becomes their sacred altar and sexual intercourse their sacrament, because they are fulfilling God's will. They are also using that gift in an unselfish way, for the good of the other.

Pornography, on the other hand, takes what is sacred and holy in the safe container of committed love, separates it, objectifies it, displays it on glossy paper or a computer screen, and drives those who secretly indulge in its dark pleasure into isolation, loneliness, shame, despair and sometimes even death. Too often I have heard the anguish of those struggling with this addiction, fearful of being caught, needing help to overcome it, yet too ashamed and afraid to reach out for help. Pornography uses/abuses the gift of sexuality for a selfish end only, just the opposite of Jesus who, as mentioned earlier, refused to use his divine power for any self-serving purpose.

So where is the spirituality in all of this? The whole schema is our spiritual life, which can be lived positively, in a healthy way, or negatively, in an unhealthy way. The way we look after ourselves physically, use our intellect, deal with our emotions, relate to God through prayer and worship, relate to others with forgiveness and understanding, relate to ourselves with self-acceptance, relate to all of God's creation through a caring ecology, and especially, respect and treat our human sexuality, submitting it to God's will – all of this is our spiritual life, positive or negative. Thus, the drunk in a gutter is just as spiritual a person as you or me, only living out his or her spirituality in an unhealthy way.

Elvis Presley, Janice Joplin, Amy Winehouse, Michael Jackson, Philip Seymour Hoffman, Robin Williams, Prince and others have one thing in common – all died prematurely, either at their own hand or as a result of their actions. Hoffman, for one, was found dead on the bathroom floor of his New York apartment with a syringe in his left arm. The New York medical examiner's office stated he died of acute mixed drug intoxication, including heroin, cocaine, benzodiazepines and amphetamine. For all of these people, we can ask, "Why?"

I do not judge them, but I suspect they perhaps did not look after themselves physically, were probably very intelligent but made some bad decisions, did not know how to handle their emotions, struggled in their relationship with God and others, struggled with low self-worth or low self-esteem, and also struggled with their sexuality. Janis Joplin remarked that she went out on stage, made love to five thousand people, and was supposed to sleep alone? No wonder she consumed alcohol before each performance. In *All of Me,* a book about her life, Anne Murray says she was shocked to discover that Dusty Springfield, whom she considered the best Caucasian female singer of her time, struggled with low self-esteem, and perhaps died prematurely because of that struggle.

On the other hand, St. Mother Teresa of Calcutta, a celibate religious woman, had tremendous energy, a tremendous Eros that she handled very positively. Even though she experienced the apparent absence of God during much of her ministry, she founded and joyfully ran an international congregation, ministered to the destitute and dying of Calcutta, was awarded the Nobel Peace Prize, and was given a state funeral in India. She handled the tension of living positively her human incompleteness very well indeed.

The Spiritual Spiral

The image about heaven I recall permeating my youth was a ladder I was struggling to climb one rung at a time, often slipping off and having to get back on by going to confession. By my late teens it was becoming a boring, lifeless pattern, and I remember wondering if that was all there was to this life of faith and spirituality.

During a retreat one year, that all changed for me. The retreat master simply drew three circles in a spiral moving upwards on a flip chart, then talked about how we change and grow through the Paschal Mystery. Something inside me immediately connected with this explanation, and I felt new hope and excitement about my faith and ministry. That spiral image has influenced my growth and healing. It has also become a healing instrument I can share with others.

As I reflected on this image, it struck me that Jewish spirituality is the line (the Abrahamic journey) with a beginning and a destination. Indigenous spirituality is the circle (the Medicine Wheel): cyclical, seasonal, inclusive, with direction and movement. What Judeo-Christian spirituality has done is put the two together to create the Spiritual Spiral – a line moving upwards with circles of diminishing size connected to it underneath – creating a continuous passion-death-resurrection scenario.

It is lived out in this way:

> When we come face to face with a painful truth about ourselves, down we go into our passion.

As we deal with that dark reality through prayer, sharing and self-awareness, we hit bottom, let it go and die to it. And as we are filled by the Holy Spirit with that defect's opposite virtue and the feeling of serenity, we rise not to the same place we were before, but to the top of the next, smaller circle, poised to go through this Paschal Mystery again if and when we need to. It is an exciting, never-ending journey of personal growth and inner healing.

Living the Spiritual Spiral

That spirituality soon manifested itself in my life in fairly dramatic ways. A first way happened when I did some impatient speeding on dusty gravel roads while taking someone to the hospital. It wasn't an emergency, but I used the situation as an excuse to pass a vehicle, with dust and rocks flying. What I didn't know was the new administrator of the hospital in one of the missions was in the vehicle, very angry and frightened by that incident. Upon her arrival, she was telling the sisters at the hospital about a "maniac in a green car" who had passed her on the road, when she glanced out the window, spotted me and exclaimed, "That's him!"

I was found out, and I was mortified when told about this a few weeks later. My reaction, interestingly, matched the stages of dying that Elisabeth Kübler-Ross wrote about in *On Death and Dying*: denial, anger, bargaining, depression and acceptance. I went into denial, blaming the person for not pulling over and letting me by sooner. I felt angry at being caught and for what she labelled me. I spent a month and a half in a restless state of bargaining, questioning, blaming, rationalizing, avoiding, until I realized I was carrying a rather depressing burden of guilt and fear, and would carry it forever if I did not do something about it.

Finally, I arrived at acceptance. I sat down and wrote her a letter, acknowledged what I had done, accepted responsibility for it, and apologized. I had to question why I had acted that way, and then wondered if I might have an addictive personality. Further to that, I realized I was right back at step one of the Twelve Step program I had begun a year earlier – powerless over my character defect of impatience, for which I needed healing as much as forgiveness for my reckless driving. Working these steps with the focus on my impatience was how I would heal and grow.

The final connection was with the Spiritual Spiral. Passion, death and resurrection was what working these steps would lead me through. My passion was facing the painful truth about myself, my impatience. My death was hitting bottom, wanting to change, sharing my powerlessness, praying I would be able to let it go, and my resurrection was the healing of my impatience I received through that process.

Another example that happened around the same time focused on my stubbornness. The first year of ministry was an experience of first fervour for me, including my dream of forming that basic Christian community I mentioned earlier.

Garry, a Métis teacher, was part of that initiative. He lived with me in the small rectory. After six months of this experience, Garry left with no explanation. When he returned to visit a few months later, I asked him why he left our fledgling community. He replied it was because I was stubborn. Immediately, those stages of dying kicked in again. I denied it, claiming I was strong willed and knew what we needed to do to form community. He stood his ground and insisted I was stubborn; I always got my way.

Then my anger surfaced at him for daring to come to my house and accuse me of this personal shortcoming. Sensing my anger, he left much earlier than he had planned. I did not sleep well that night, bargaining and arguing with myself about whether he was right or wrong. The next morning, I woke up depressed, feeling sorry for myself. I called the school to excuse myself from teaching Christian Ethics. Then there was a knock on the door. It was Jim, head of DNS Resources for Northern Saskatchewan and a member of the charismatic prayer group in his community. He was in town for a meeting.

When he introduced himself and asked how I was doing, I told him, "Terrible. I just found out I am stubborn!" He offered to pray over me, which I accepted. He prayed for "liberation from rigidity and domination," which shocked me a little. We went for lunch, then he went to his meeting. I felt miserable for the whole weekend. On Monday I decided to go to a local family's cottage at the lake for a *poustinia* (a twenty-four-hour retreat of fasting and prayer).

At noon during that retreat, sitting on the shore, I took a cup of water out of the lake to drink (it is a spring-fed lake) and thought – the lake is twenty kilometres long and five kilometres wide. I just took a cup of water out of it and the lake won't even notice the difference. Then it struck me: that lake is God's love; this cup is my stubbornness. Suddenly I felt a weight lift off my shoulders and peace flooding my spirit. There was a healing of my stubbornness.

> The key to this spiral is the circles get smaller (dealing with our issues gets easier each time) and the line is always going up (we are always healing). So, growth and healing, being still green and growing, happens through all these methods – the stages of dying, the Twelve Step program, and the Spiritual Spiral of passion, death and resurrection.

4

Companions on a Journey

Life is a journey in which we discover ourselves in discovering God, and discover God in discovering our true self hidden in God.

—James Finley

The Importance of Spiritual Direction

As is perhaps the case with most contemporary Catholics, spiritual direction was not even on the horizon for me as a young person until I entered the Oblate novitiate in Arnprior, Ontario, where the late Fr. Don McCleod OMI visited weekly to share a spiritual talk and meet with the novices one on one.

Even then I didn't take it seriously until I asked Adam Exner, mentioned earlier, to be my spiritual director. When we began, the first thing he said was that if he was going to direct me, he would have to know me. He invited me to tell him my story. I was somewhat taken aback, as I didn't think I had any story to tell, but when he told me just to talk about my life and family starting as far back as I could remember, I talked for an hour!

After a second hour-long session, he gave me what proved to be life-changing feedback. He suggested I needed to work on my relationship with my father (would that I had taken his advice more seriously at the time) and pray with Isaiah 43:1-4 for a whole month.

That passage, which I read for the first time in my Jerusalem Bible, stunned me. I heard God speaking to me these words: "Sylvain, do not fear. I have called you by name, you are mine. Should you walk through fire, you won't be burned; should you pass through rivers, you won't drown. I give Egypt, Ethiopia and Seba for you." Above all, I heard God say to me, "Sylvain, you are precious and honoured in my sight because I love you."

There it was in black and white – I was precious and honoured in God's sight, not because of anything I had done, but simply because God loved me! For years I had been trying to earn my father's love (and indirectly trying to earn God's love without being aware of it), and it wasn't working. I felt massive relief and gratitude, and closer to God than ever before.

> Experiencing God's love, being loved by God, did not depend on anything I had ever done or would do. This was a powerful experience of unconditional love.

It was transformational, and the beginning of my life-long healing journey.

I have had many spiritual directors over the years, whose wisdom and guidance I truly cherish and for which I am grateful. However, it is only now, as I am doing spiritual direction as a main part of my ministry, that I am able to appreciate the power, wonder, awe, gratitude, delight and joy involved in journeying with another person along their pilgrim way. At times, I find myself moved to the very depths of my being.

For me, the role of a spiritual director involves first of all being on a healing journey ourselves, listening with attention to the other's story, discerning how the Holy Spirit is active in that person's life, encouraging and affirming the progress they are making, challenging them whenever necessary without judgment, and trying to connect faith and scripture with the person's life.

Sharing a Spiritual Journey

As an illustration of the importance of spiritual direction on one's healing journey, I have obtained permission to share with you an elderly woman's exceptional spiritual journey. We will call her Delores.

In her late seventies, Delores attended a retreat I was giving on addictions awareness that stirred up a lot of unresolved issues from her past. Sensing she needed help to deal with this challenge, Delores decided to resume journeying with a spiritual director for this last stage of her life and asked if I could be that person.

During our first session, I asked her to begin by sharing what was going on in her family while she was in her mother's womb. The reason for starting there is my belief that babies in the womb are influenced by what is happening outside the womb, positively or negatively. An important part of our story is the time we spent in our mother's womb and what was happening in our home during that time. I also find it helpful to get a picture of the family setting into which the person is born, so that was where we began.

Not surprisingly, there was tension in Delores's home from a rigid, demanding father and a mother who withheld affection, so the seeds of dysfunction were already planted when she was in the womb. Delores's story also surfaced some deep-seated wounds from her father's strict discipline and punishment for some misdemeanours, often leaving welts on her legs.

A more pressing matter that surfaced, however, was her struggle to cope with another resident living in the same seniors' residence who was abusive to her. As she put it, she needed help to cope with this person who for some reason had it in for her and who would cross her path often. This person seemed full of insecurity, anger, hurt, at times rage, perfectionism, control, and fear. Delores read Jesuit Fr. Govan's book *All Is Gift*, which helped her cope somewhat with this very difficult person. This promised to be an interesting and challenging journey. How she handled this challenge in a marvellous fashion will be discussed in a later chapter.

After our first few sessions, Delores began to journal like never before. She became aware of her defects of character, especially her anger, false pride, being critical and her tendency to judge others. Delores shared how she sometimes felt too old and that it was too late to be on this healing journey, yet something in her yearned for it. I suggested she pay attention to that yearning. She wondered if all the falling apart she was doing would ever come together again. That question reminded me of Dr. Dabrowski, one of our professors at Newman Theological College, and his theory of Positive Disintegration. I shared with her his teaching that many things in our lives have to disintegrate or fall apart so something new can be born.

At one point in between sessions, she wrote,

Thank you for your listening ear and heart, for receiving whatever I said no matter what I said or how it was said. Today I seem to be walking around in kind of a daze …

a sort of numbness ... I think something needs to settle inside of me as a result of yesterday ... or is there more to 'erupt'? ... I was hoping I would feel peaceful and rather joyful but that is not the case. I don't even feel relief. It seems like there are lots of tears inside to be shed but they won't come out ... they seem to be stuck. For now, I am just sort of letting things be ... it's quite a journey into the unknown. In time, the Spirit will lead me to wherever I need to be led ... but I feel like saying enough for now!!! Just leave me alone!!! Please keep praying for me in this journey.

Paying Attention to Dreams

Often, Delores would come with a dream, and at times, numerous dreams. I always invited her to share them. I am convinced that God, as he did with many biblical figures, has been speaking to her in her dreams. We tried to discern what God may be trying to tell her through her dreams. Without fail, every one of her dreams over a span of two years related to her personal spiritual journey of growth and healing.

At the beginning of our sessions, her dreams were darker, involving things like being stuck, loss, running into obstacles, and so on. In one of her earliest dreams, Delores dreamt of losing a black purse and finding a brown purse, as well as driving a car. I suggested the black purse was what she had already let go of, the brown purse was the issues still facing her, and driving a car was an affirmation of the healing journey on which she had embarked.

At one point she wrote, "I am so glad we are working with my dreams ... so helpful to me. Every session with you spurs me on deeper and deeper. Since yesterday I somehow feel much lighter inside and more peace-filled, just being, I guess, and thankful to you and to God for all that is happening within."

One dream especially touched on some deep issues in her life. She dreamt she was in a hallway, this time on the bottom floor. She saw a creature wrapped in a new green covering. She suspected there was a person inside. She was afraid at first, but overcame her fear, touched the creature, and started to unwrap it. She found a boy around fifteen years old inside with a gun. She asked for the gun, which he handed over to her without hesitation.

At first, I saw this as a statement about where she was situated on her healing journey (the hallway), having gone to the bottom of her issues, and having overcome her fears. The new green colour represented her growth and healing, and the boy her True Self. The gun may represent her fears she has faced and overcome.

Then Delores shared some concern as to why she was so abrupt and rude at times. She went on to mention being kicked by her brother, strapped occasionally by her dad, yelled at, sometimes punished when the children were noisy during a hockey game their dad was listening to on the radio, and said her mother was sometimes verbally abusive. She felt rejected, became very shy, and when she was very young often tried to hide when visitors came to the house.

I realized this dream was not a statement, but an invitation to go deeper (the hallway on the bottom floor) into these past hurts, to remember them, to feel and stay with the feelings she has repressed all these years. That was how she could begin to truly love herself. Finally, I suggested she empty herself of these emotions by writing to each hurtful person and communicating her feelings with love as a way of trying to forgive them (again, a process to be discussed later).

In another dream, she was lying under a tree. Her brother was on a branch and dropped a squirrel in front of her. It was in bad shape and could hardly lift up its head. Then he dropped three dead kittens and she woke up.

My interpretation was that she was the squirrel, in diminished shape, getting older and weaker. The number three represented the days Jesus spent in the tomb. She had to live the Spiritual Spiral – die to clinging to her physical health and ability to do things and practise a spirituality of letting go. She needed to be at peace with aging and learn to just be, rather than always doing. I shared with her my joy visiting my ninety-two-year-old aunt who could do little, but whom I knew was praying for me. The dream was a call for her to be like my aunt.

Another dream placed her in a seniors' residence similar to the one where she was living. She checked the doors to be sure they were secure. Two had deadbolts and one did not. She was talking with others when they heard the latter door being jiggled open. She got up to check and saw a man there, someone she knew. He left when he saw her, and then she woke up.

To me, this dream built on previous dreams. Delores has arrived at a place of rest, peace and serenity, being at home. The doors with deadbolts were issues she has resolved; the door that jiggled open represented some smaller issues still needing to be looked at, as did the man who appeared and left. Again, the dream reflects her progress on her spiritual journey.

Delores's more recent dreams had her looking for a variety of different objects. After some discussion, we discerned what she was really looking for was intimacy. All her life, Dolores had never really experienced intimacy within her family and within her present situation. She did have a fairly close friend in a city not too far away, so I invited her to develop that friendship and allow it to mature into a more trusting relationship that would give her an experience of greater intimacy, mirroring the intimacy God wants to have with her (the focus of a separate chapter).

There is an element of Radical Discipleship in her life (also to be discussed later), as she realizes she is getting older, weaker and unable to do many things she did before. She counted her blessings, all the things she can still do, and was grateful, as many are worse off. Then she wrote about accepting what she could not do and being ready to let go of more things in the future, which I readily affirmed.

Delores's amazing, grace-filled and intriguing journey, among many others, is why I find doing spiritual direction so fulfilling and energizing, even if at times demanding and challenging. I believe a counsellor should be in counselling him- or herself, and a spiritual director should also be in spiritual direction him- or herself.

I would encourage especially those of us in our second half of life to consider taking some formation and becoming spiritual directors, privileged to share our wisdom gained over the years, as part of this rewarding and life-giving ministry.

5

Why Am I Afraid to Love You – and Myself?

Those who have finally learned to love
find themselves absurdly happy,
totally involved, tragically vulnerable,
and always in trouble.

—Author unknown

Sharing Life's Hurts

She approached quietly, timidly, unsure of just what she was looking for, or why she came to talk, for her original intention in coming to the church that morning during the parish mission was to pray before the Blessed Sacrament. But I was there, alone and available in the dimly lit church, so she came. I was grateful in the end that she did, for we had a heart-to-heart sharing in which she was able to bare her soul and reach out for help.

She was one of the few persons in all of my ministry who was able to admit that her greatest sin was she did not love herself. Born into a dysfunctional family, sexually abused repeatedly as a child, and now in an abusive relationship, she told me she was a nobody, a non-person, of no importance, or at least that was how she saw and felt about herself. All that was keeping her going was having a key to the church, where she came each day to pray for strength and consolation.

My heart melted within me as I heard her plaintive cry and I was moved with compassion. I invited her to rejoice, for at least she was being humble, admitting her reality, naming it, sharing it, and in that process, was finally beginning to love herself. Her next step was to start believing how much God, her creator, loved her, was crazy about her, delighted in her. As I had been instructed to do by my spiritual director decades earlier, I invited her to pray with Isaiah 43:1-4, to ponder and believe the words of God telling her she was precious and honoured in God's eyes because God loved her.

I could not pour God's love into her – I could only try to get her to believe there was nothing she could do to make God love her more than God already does. I also reminded her she was not alone – St. Augustine was in a similar place at one point when he expressed in his *Confessions*, "Late have I loved you, beauty so old and so new: late have I loved you. … You called and cried out loud and you shattered my deafness." The words of another saint, Abbot Bernard, speaking about Jesus and his mother, Mary, were also helpful: "He died in body through a love greater than anyone had known; she died in spirit through a love unlike any other since his" (Office of Readings, Octave of Assumption, September 15). And since the woman I met in the church that day was such a prayerful person, I think she needed to ponder the words of John 3:16: "For God so loved the world that he gave his only Son, so that everyone who believes in him may have eternal life." She needed to be grounded more deeply in God's love for her.

Our Need to Love and Be Loved

In a public lecture back in the early '70s, I heard the late Dr. Glasser of Reality Therapy fame speak of "met" and "unmet" needs as the source of our wellness or dis-ease. He mentioned a hierarchy of needs including freedom, leisure, a certain amount of power, love, laughter, education, and more. For the purposes of the workshops and retreats I conduct, I boiled all these needs down to three: the need to be loved, belong and be valued.

One morning a phone call came to the rectory from a woman who wanted me to visit her alcoholic husband, who was recovering from a hangover. When I arrived, he was sitting on the couch, muttering to himself, "Nobody loves me, nobody loves me." His wife and three children were present and very concerned, but he was unable to see or accept their love. His parents were alcoholics – one had frozen to death, while the other died of alcohol poisoning. He had never received or experienced the love he needed as a child; now, as an adult and successful fisherman, he could not perceive or accept his family's love for him. He simply could not see himself as loved and loveable.

> Our need to belong is another deep-seated, powerful need. We need to feel we are part of something bigger than us, to which we are connected and by which we feel accepted.

Cathy, a resident in a youth detention centre, was being beaten up by a motorcycle gang. When asked why she hung around with those guys, she replied simply and predictably, "I have to belong somewhere." Life becomes intolerable if we feel we don't belong, and some people will put up with abuse and demeaning behaviour just to belong.

A third, somewhat overlooked, human need is to be valued, to feel wanted and appreciated: to know that our life and person make a difference to others, that people will miss us when we are gone. The same young woman, Cathy, was caught flushing her medication down the toilet. When told she needed the medication to live, she replied defiantly, "I don't care." Those are terrible words when we stop to think about them – not caring whether we live or die, not feeling valued.

Grounded in Love

St. Paul, in his letter to the Ephesians, writes eloquently about love: "I pray that, according to the riches of his glory, [God] may grant that you may be strengthened in your inner being with power through his Spirit, and that Christ may dwell in your hearts through faith, as you are being rooted and grounded in love" (Ephesians 3:16-17).

Traditionally, there are four kinds of love: *storge, philia, eros* and *agape*.[19]

Storge has the meaning of affection or fondness through familiarity [a brotherly love], especially between family members or people who have otherwise found themselves together by chance. It is described as the most natural, emotive, and widely diffused of loves – 'natural' in that it is present without coercion; 'emotive' because it is the result of fondness due to familiarity; and most 'widely diffused' because it pays the least attention to those characteristics deemed 'valuable' or worthy of love and, as a result, is able to transcend most discriminating factors.

Philia or friendship is the strong bond existing between people who have a common interest or activity. Friendship is the least biological, organic, instinctive, gregarious and necessary ... the least *natural* of loves – our species does not need friendship in order to reproduce – but to the classical and medieval worlds, the more profound precisely because it is freely chosen. Some would claim the ancient world had a much greater appreciation for friendship than exists today.

Eros is a more romantic love, a chemistry, an attraction to someone or something, sometimes confused with the sense of "being in love." It is often an extremely profound experience that can be expressed both positively or negatively, for good or for ill, and in that sense is neutral in and of itself. As we have seen earlier, it flows from our being created *imago Dei*, in the image and likeness of God, and thus is a divine fire within us seeking expression, completion and consummation.

Agape is unconditional love that brings forth caring regardless of the circumstance. This is the greatest of loves, and a specifically Christian virtue. It supersedes all the other more natural loves and sees them as very much secondary to this love of God and God-like love. It is the experience of this love alone that can truly satisfy the deepest yearnings of the human heart, leading to the joy only God can give.

The World's First and Greatest Psychologist

No one could be more attuned to our human needs, or more aware of how these needs are met, than the one who created us with them.

That is why Jesus gave us the Great Commandment in the gospels (Matthew 22:34-40). Knowing our need to be loved, he first of all commands us to love God, because God is love and loves us unconditionally. All we have to do is love God back through prayer and worship, and our need to be loved will to a great extent be met.

Next, knowing we need to belong, Jesus commands us to love others – that is, learn to accept them as they are, understand them, forgive them, trust them, care for them, share life with them – and our need to belong will be met.

Lastly, knowing we need to be valued, Jesus instructs us to love ourselves – learn to forgive ourselves our mistakes, accept ourselves as we are, be less hard on ourselves, take greater care of ourselves, and our need to be valued will be met.

How Are We to Love?

For some time now, I have found it opportune and helpful to summarize this commandment to love as a continuum of five different levels: we are to love God with our whole being, love others, love ourselves, love one another as Jesus has loved us (John 15:12), and finally, love even our enemies (Matthew 5:44).

The last two levels raise the bar infinitely high – to love others as Jesus has loved us is to be ready to give our lives for others in a sacrificial love just like his. And to love our enemies is best accomplished by forgiving them and praying for them, as Jesus did on the cross. As he himself put it, there can be no greater love than this. Nor is there a greater challenge than this, one that much of the rest of this book will be dedicated to addressing.

Removing Our Blinders

As we have seen, it is difficult to love God and love others if we do not love ourselves – if we think that when it comes to us, God has made junk. Perhaps a personal experience will illustrate this best.

In 1976, two years after being ordained a priest, I attended a retreat for clergy. As I was walking outside with someone during a break, Fr. Vince approached us, walking with another retreatant. When he looked up and saw me, he cheerfully greeted me with the words "Gee, Sylvain, it's great to see your face again," to which I replied without thinking, "Sure, if you don't have anything better to look at."

He winced, a hurt look flashing across his face, and said quietly, "I do, when I look in a mirror," then kept on walking. I felt small, like crawling under the pavement, ashamed, and confused – why had I uttered that pitiful response? Where did it come from? Yet I had spoken it – the words were out, had been heard, done their damage and could not be taken back. I felt like beating myself up and found it hard to concentrate on the retreat for the next few days.

Eventually, as I reflected and pondered on this painful incident, it dawned on me that I was struggling with low self-esteem, low self-worth, and ultimately, a lack of self-love. I was having a hard time loving myself, even as an ordained priest. I did not believe Vince when he spoke those affirming words, and so I pushed away his love. I was breaking one of the commandments Jesus gave us – to love ourselves. Eventually, I knew I had to learn to love myself. I have been working on that ever since.

Part of loving myself involved accepting the fact I was going bald, something I tried to hide for many months by letting my hair grow longer and combing it over the balding area. Of course, that did not work, as the wind kept blowing it back! One day, my barber gave me a short haircut and told me to accept it – it was the Blaze look! I was somewhat shocked, but her radical action did help me to accept reality. I also had to learn to accept compliments and not denigrate them. I have made much progress, although at times some of that old behaviour and attitude tries to sneak back in. What helps is remembering that loving ourselves is a commandment we are to keep and live.

What Is Our Way of Being?

Another word for loving oneself is self-awareness, knowing oneself.

As Rohr put it at the beginning of a retreat conference, "You are who you are who you are – what are you afraid of?" That comment almost knocked me out of my chair as a young Oblate at the time, because I was afraid of myself, and thought if others really got to know me, they wouldn't like me – not a comfortable place to be. Eventually, we should be able to answer the question "What is our way of being?" Again, an incident will serve to illustrate.

In 2005, I was in training in Morley, Alberta, to become a facilitator for the Returning to Spirit (RTS) program that was just beginning at the time. The instructor and co-founder of the program was Mark Pizandawatc, who at one point asked us to articulate our Way of Being. As I understand it now, that is our habitual way of thinking, feeling and acting in the world, the way we comport ourselves in our daily lives.

One participant in particular was struggling to identify her Way of Being. Mark offered to help her, and she accepted. When he suggested "Drama Queen," she reacted with indignation, but the rest of the class erupted in laughter because he had nailed it. That was the way we perceived she was – everything about her had to be dramatic and done with flair. She was not ready to hear what to her was a painful truth, but eventually settled down, admitted the truth of that view and was able to accept it, work with it and make changes in her way of living.

This bothered me because I was also struggling to identify and articulate my Way of Being. Shortly after that incident, I had to drop out of the program when I was named a bishop. However, that unanswered question continued to bother me until I visited one of our communities where the pastor, in his introduction of me to the community, happened to mention, "We Oblates call him Mr. Fix-It." I was shocked and tried not to react, but I wondered why he had used that label. Upon further reflection, I came to appreciate that comment, because I realized he had just named my Way of Being. I truly was "Mr. Fix-It," especially as a young priest trying to solve and fix everyone's problem in a community of five hundred faithful. No wonder I almost burned out after my first year of ministry.

And now I was faced with the painful truth that even in my first year as a bishop in the second half of life, the tendency to be a fixer was lingering and visible to others. It wasn't a pleasant truth, but now, aware of it like that participant in the RTS workshop, I could choose to humbly accept it and work on myself to change, heal, become more easy-going and less fixated on fixing others. And that led to greater freedom and less stress in my life. I was now beginning to love myself more and live that commandment Jesus gave us. My senior years would thus be more mature and more rewarding than those earlier years of ministry, and that was truly a gift.

Living in Harmony and Balance

To sum all this up and link faith with our human needs, there are three essential pillars for a life of harmony and balance: faith, fellowship and self-awareness.

> Our need to be loved is all about faith, our need to belong is all about fellowship, and our need to be valued is all about self-awareness. The commandment to love God and allow God to love us is all about faith, the commandment to love others is all about fellowship, and the commandment to love ourselves is all about self-awareness.

Ultimately, living the commandments Jesus gave us will help us have our human needs met and live a fully human life of harmony and balance.

Incidentally, the Twelve Step program of Alcoholics Anonymous (which anyone can use for their own growth and healing) resonates perfectly with this spiritual perspective: four of the steps (2, 3, 7, 11) are all about faith (belief, surrender and prayer); four (5, 8, 9, 12) are all about fellowship (confession of wrongdoing, making amends and sharing one's spiritual experience) and four (1, 4, 6, 10) are all about self-awareness (powerlessness, moral inventory, listing defects of character and a daily review of one's behaviour). Those belonging to a fellowship and working the steps will automatically live the Great Commandment and find their basic human needs met as they experience a new life of sobriety, joyous and free.

6

The Lifeline of Intimacy

The temptation of power is greatest when intimacy is a threat.
Much Christian leadership is exercised by people who do not
know how to develop healthy, intimate relationships and
have opted for power and control instead.

—*Henri Nouwen*

This insightful and cryptic comment by Henri Nouwen
alone can be motivation to explore the role of love as
intimacy in our lives, especially as we age, and the danger
we all face of slipping into the false gods of power and control
if we are afraid of it, as he points out. This chapter will do just
that, with this reflection by Nouwen serving as a backdrop to our
exploration.

Why the Oblates?

When I was a student and wondering what God wanted me to do
with my life, I had many options. Because deep within my being I
could not see myself married (the late Kelly Nemeck OMI, director
of the Leb Shemeah House of Prayer, called that being essentially
"unmarriageable"), yet aware I needed a lifetime commitment,

I began to discern a vocation to the priesthood. The choice was between a more individualistic diocesan priesthood or joining a religious community.

The final decision was to join the Missionary Oblates of Mary Immaculate, a decision I have never regretted. Why that choice? Could it be I was seeking a larger family, a deeper sense of belonging and community, the experience of relationships that might be more fulfilling than what family had provided thus far, or feeling an inchoate need for more powerful male bonding?

There may not be a clear answer to that question, but I know this – I always hoped for, and in gentle ways attempted to facilitate, a deeper level of sharing among us as brother Oblates. I remember feeling excitement when a few Oblate leaders tried to bring about sharing groups, and disappointment when these attempts never got off the ground.

Early Ventures into Intimacy

As mentioned earlier, my first attempt at establishing a basic Christian community did not succeed because I was our own worst enemy – my workaholism and pace of life never allowed a genuine community to emerge.

On the other hand, when Tom, a young man who was interested in the Oblates, came to stay for a summer, we were able to do a version of what I called "night sharing" that I had learned from Armand Nigro SJ on a thirty-day retreat before my ordination. Each night, we would spend some time sharing a word from scripture, our experience of the day, our feelings, and praying for each other's needs. That experience was very life-giving for both of us, and it seems to have been instrumental in this young man becoming an Oblate brother who still ministers to immigrants, Indigenous people and the inner-city poor.

Another incident that helped me experience the power of fellowship was joining the movement of Alcoholics Anonymous just starting up in our community at the time, even if I was not an alcoholic. I had been attending the meetings as pastor to give a spiritual talk, but after a year of frustrating ministry trying to change a whole community, I wanted the freedom and joy these humble recovering addicts were obviously experiencing. With the chairperson's encouragement, I overcame my hesitation and made the decision to join the group at the next meeting.

When invited to share, I said, "My name is Sylvain, I'm a friend of alcoholics, and I want to join the group." Although I was afraid of rejection, for the first time ever I shared my personal struggle and my feelings with a group of about twelve people that night, instead of giving my usual spiritual talk. As we closed with the Our Father, my knees were shaking and my hands were sweating. I just stood there, eyes closed and motionless, when someone shook my hand. Another person gave me a cup of coffee, and then I felt it – a powerful, joyful surge of acceptance and belonging. I was in – part of the group!

Reflecting on that experience, I realized that trusting the group as I did, and being listened to by each one present, was a profound experience of intimacy and love. We were living the words of St. Paul in 1 Corinthians 13:9:

Love is always ready to trust and to accept whatever comes.

I had trusted them and they had silently accepted me. I was being loved into new life by this experience of intimate fellowship and powerful belonging.

In 1978, another Oblate and I did a Marriage Encounter as the odd couple and eventually became team priests. On a long trip after the weekend, we dialogued on the ninety questions we were given, and we continued to dialogue whenever we met. That experience of dialogue helped us grow in self-awareness, and also probably saved his life, as both his addiction and his illness surfaced through our dialogue. Our sharing led him to join AA, seek a diagnosis and accept treatment for his life-threatening illness.

When our first attempt at basic Christian community with the Grey Nuns and lay persons in my first mission did not materialize, the two sisters and I began to "trialogue" after the Marriage Encounter they had also attended. Every Friday we would lock the doors to the convent, sit around the oak table upstairs, do some faith sharing based on scripture, share our feelings, pray for each other's needs and end with a board game. This trialogue process continued for four years, leading to healing and growth on the part of each of us, but especially for one sister, who gained confidence and lost her stutter. It was truly delightful and exciting to see these two women religious, living in community together for years and now in the second half of life, experience genuine intimacy for the first time.

Friendship in the Lord

Judith Viorst, in her book *Necessary Losses*, writes:

> Close friends contribute to our personal growth. They also contribute to our personal pleasure, making the music sound sweeter, the wine taste richer, the laughter ring louder because they are there. Friends furthermore take care – they come if we call them at two in the morning; they lend us their car, their bed, their money, their ear; and although no contracts are written, it is clear that intimate friendships involve important rights and obligations. Indeed, we will frequently turn – for reassurance, for

comfort, for come-and-save-me help – not to our blood relations but to friends, to intimate friends ....[20]

A powerful biblical model of friendship is that of Jonathan and David in the Old Testament (1 Samuel 18:1, 20:17). A more contemporary model for us would be Bishop Gregory Nazianzen and his close friend St. Basil. Here is a description of their friendship taken from a sermon delivered by Gregory and found in the Office of Readings:

> Our studies were the prelude to our friendship, the kindling of that flame that was to bind us together. In this way we began to feel affection for each other. When, in the course of time, we acknowledged our friendship and recognized that our ambition was a life of true wisdom, we became everything to each other. We shared the same lodging, the same table, the same desires, the same goal. Our love for each other grew daily warmer and deeper. The same hope inspired us: the pursuit of learning. This is an ambition especially subject to envy. Yet between us there was no envy. On the contrary, we made capital out of our rivalry. Our rivalry consisted, not in seeking the first place for oneself, but in yielding it to the other, for we each looked on the other's success as his own. We seemed to be two bodies with a single spirit. Though we cannot believe those who claim that everything is contained in everything, yet you must believe that in our case each of us was in the other and with the other.[21]

Along that same line, a poster on a wall at a treatment centre for addictions caught my attention: "A true friend is like a diamond, precious and rare. False friends are like autumn leaves, found everywhere."

How true – a friend in need is a friend indeed. A friend in whom one can trust, who is loyal and committed to the friendship come what may, who will help us find our Way of Being, who is there when needed and whose company one can enjoy when not needed is a priceless gift.

I used to give a unique spiritual talk on friendship during our Christopher Leadership courses. In crafting it, I looked back over my life and thought of all the friends I enjoyed along the way, and the particular gift they were for me or the particular life lesson they taught me. Then I rolled them all into one fictional person and pretended that person was present but hidden from the audience. The talk was structured as an introduction to that person who would give the real talk instead of me. After listing all the qualities of that imaginary composite friend, I would ask the audience to please help me welcome ... Jesus Christ!

That is what Jesus called us in John 15:14-15: "You are my friends if you do what I command you. I do not call you servants any longer, because the servant does not know what the master is doing; but I have called you friends, because I have made known to you everything that I have heard from my Father."

While that is wonderful good news and a very consoling truth,

Incarnational spirituality means it is up to us to put flesh to those words – to be that kind of friend to each other in daily life and reality.

John was experiencing clinical depression, and was in the third month of a five-month process of therapy without making much progress. At some point Michael, another resident in the program, befriended him and invited John to accompany him on a trip back to his hometown. That journey, the sharing of stories, doing a bit of sightseeing and meeting Michael's friend did as much to bring John out of his depression as the past months of therapy. John started to come alive, feel new energy, and want to get up in the morning: he realized his depression was starting to lift simply because someone else noticed him, took an interest in him and affirmed his existence – in short, became his friend.

Their friendship continued after John's treatment ended and became a commitment for life. Eventually, it was Michael's turn to become severely depressed when some financial woes hit him hard, and now it was John who was there for him – phoning often, encouraging him and praying hard for him, helping him through his personal crisis that bordered on taking his own life. Although living thousands of kilometres apart in separate countries, they are in weekly contact by phone, and John manages to find a way to visit Michael whenever he can. Both are very grateful to God and to each other for that priceless gift of friendship.

Intimacy as Participating in the Divine

At a Marriage Encounter Deeper Training weekend I attended, a woman responded to the question "How does it make me feel when I achieve intimacy with my spouse?" with this answer: "It feels like there are no walls, no boundaries, and no separation between us." As I heard her articulate these words, it struck me she was talking about salvation. She was experiencing eternal life now, in her relationship with her husband.

What prompted me to arrive at that conclusion was the promise Jesus makes in chapter 14 of the gospel of John to reveal himself to those who love him (verses 21-23). That promise had me intrigued and puzzled for a long time until I heard this woman's answer. Then suddenly it all made sense: when a couple trust each other completely, forgive each other everything, have no secrets between them, they truly fully consummate their marriage and become one as God is one. They experience God in their intimate relationship because they not only mirror but also participate in the intimate relationship of the Trinity.

Imagine that divine relationship – the energy, love and intimacy flowing from Father to Son and from the Son to the Spirit and in turn from the Spirit to the Father – the *perichoresis* or divine circle dance mentioned earlier. Achieving intimacy in their relationship is probably the best way a husband and wife can experience God, who reveals God's self to them, in their marriage. The outcome is joyful, even blissful communion. During a Marriage Encounter fiftieth-anniversary convention, Fran shared after a trialogue with her husband, Frank, and me that she had just "tasted heaven."

Not only married couples, but also any truly intimate relationship of soulmates of any gender, if bonded by humble, honest trust and acceptance within safe boundaries, can experience the same relationship with the Trinity. No wonder there is a small square that probably held a mirror on the front of the table in the painting of the Trinity, also known as *The Hospitality of Abraham*, by Andrei Rublev.

> We are to be the fourth person of the Trinity, participating in that divine dance not just by our intimate relationship with the three persons of the Trinity, but also with the friends and soulmates in our lives.

This dynamic also applies to families. In her book Judith Viorst includes a poignant passage from Herbert Gold's memoir-novel, *Fathers*, describing how the hero, now middle-aged, takes his daughter to a skating rink, just as his father had taken him years ago: "I remember why skating with my father gave me such joy," he writes. "It was the hope of intimacy, waiting to be redeemed ... I believed the abyss between my father and me, between others and me, could be crossed ... Like a gangster I sought to penetrate my father's secret soul. The limits remained, unredeemed."[22]

Yearning for Intimacy

These thoughts on intimacy – marital, parental and that of friends – set the stage for sharing my own venture into deeper intimacy, to which I alluded earlier. It is not without trepidation that I write these lines, but just as there was a gentle inner nudging by the Holy Spirit to join AA at one time in my life, so now that same gentle nudge is inviting me to share my experience of intimacy for the sake of a greater integrity of this book.

In the fall of 1991 I began a sabbatical year following a particularly difficult time of transition in my life. The fellow priest with whom I had worked closely and dialogued intimately for some years left because of illness, and it proved impossible to achieve the same level of intimacy with the priest who replaced him. I was experiencing a loss of intimacy in my life without fathoming the impact upon me. Without realizing it, I descended more and more into a workaholic pace of life, leaving little time for friendship. At the same time, I was given a huge responsibility I was not prepared to handle, and had to resign, one of the most painful moments of my life.

Thankfully, I was subsequently able to participate in a renewal program for priests and religious. This program allowed me time to rest and recover from all that stress. After a few months, the schedule included a Progoff Journal workshop. At one point during this event, when asked to express one of our deepest desires, I found myself saying I was yearning for intimacy. To my surprise, a few minutes later I heard another participant across the room share the exact same yearning.

As soon as the session was over, I went over to this person, who happened to be a religious sister about my age, whom I will call Sandra, and blurted out, "We're saying the same thing – we have to talk." So, we went for a walk that turned out to be the first of many and started to share our stories. Ironically, I had hardly noticed her before, as she was isolating herself due to the painful experiences she had been through before the program began.

As the weeks went by, we shared more and more, found out we had a lot in common – music, singing, art, creativity, and so on – and the trust level between us grew stronger and stronger. We shared the story of our lives, began to share our journals, and she began to come out of herself and participate in the program more. As the personal intimacy between us grew stronger, we were advised by our spiritual directors to set strong, clear boundaries, which we did.

One of the principles guiding me at that time, and helping me negotiate that powerful attraction, was the principle that guided me during my earlier Marriage Encounter years – as long as I was willing to share with another Oblate what I was sharing with anyone else, especially of the opposite gender, I was on solid ground.

I had also previously learned some lessons from a Protestant pastor who was in a therapeutic centre for clergy for acting out sexually. He was not close to his wife or his parents, but had an intimate relationship with his older brother, a paraplegic whom he had been looking after, but who had died. He had no idea why he had crossed professional boundaries as he did, but the therapist noted during a Genogram exercise of his life that it was almost a year to the day that his brother died that he began acting out in sexually abusive ways.

That was it – the reason he acted out! He was yearning for intimacy and tried to find it in a physical way. Could this tie in with that insight from Henri Nouwen about the tendency to move towards power and control that goes beyond consensual sex when intimacy is lacking in our lives? Sexual abuse, according to experts, is more about a sick need for power over an innocent human being than about pleasure.

So, there was the powerful need, and danger, of this yearning for intimacy. We need it to live a full life, yet are afraid of it because of the dangers it holds. In his book *Dark Intimacy*, David Hassel SJ claims, "there is nothing we humans crave more, fear more, and fumble more than intimacy."[23] With clear boundaries established by the end of our program, however, Sandra and I were able to set out on a life-long journey of intimate friendship in the Lord that survived the separation of many years and thousands of kilometres and continues to grow.

The Gift of Soulmates

One year, Sandra was able to come to Canada for a visit. We set out on a holiday journey we finally dubbed a "recreational, relational pilgrimage retreat" because of the way the journey unfolded. Circumstances, including a major Oblate gathering and the funeral of a brother Oblate, took us across three provinces, praying, singing, sharing, visiting Oblates and sightseeing.

On our way to the funeral, we stopped to do some sightseeing at Maligne Canyon near Jasper, Alberta. There, we walked the trail on both sides of the canyon, crossing over six bridges spanning the icy cold rushing mountain stream. As we travelled on, within the safe space of our vehicle and our clear boundaries, Sandra began to open up and share six of the more painful and even embarrassing events of her life. The bridges over Maligne Canyon became a metaphor for her healing journey and the events of her life she was sharing for the first time with anyone.

When she returned home, her counsellor was amazed at what we had done. He was so impressed by the impact that recreational, relational pilgrimage retreat had on her, he sent me a card he created himself, with a picture he had taken of a wild mountain flower on the front, and a gracious congratulatory message within affirming the power of our "friendship in the Lord" and our relationship as soulmates.

That card not only touched me deeply, it also reinforced the importance of having a trusted friend with whom one can be totally free to be oneself, and solidified my conviction that everyone, if at all possible, would benefit by having a soulmate in their life, especially as we grow older. Aging brings with it a plethora of transitions and stress that a soulmate can help us both carry and negotiate.

Meaghan Campbell, in her June 2018 *Maclean's* article on "Canada's Loneliest People," writes about the distressing reality of "elder orphans" – older people who are alone, with no family or friends, and are at risk of descending into a spiral of isolating loneliness. Some of these seniors even resort to calling 911 just to have some human contact. Emergency workers are beginning to flag some of these repeat callers and trying to find other ways of having their needs met. Just one soulmate in their lives would solve that problem.

Walking the Medicine Wheel

One day, my Oblate soulmate and I decided to visit a mission I had not been to before. On the way we prayed the rosary and walked around the Medicine Wheel, sharing how we were doing physically, what we were learning intellectually, how we had been and were feeling, how we were doing relationally with God, other people in our lives, ourselves and all of God's creation – and even how we were handling the powerful area of our human sexuality. On the way back, we celebrated Sunday Eucharist with another mission community and then made our way home.

That evening, I felt unusually mellow, serene and content. I marvelled at this feeling until my musing led me to the awareness that of course, we had achieved intimacy that day by our journey, our prayer, and especially by walking the Medicine Wheel. That was also my experience with another Oblate brother with whom I walked the Medicine Wheel while we travelled – always, there was a sense of well-being and even joy. Such is the power of achieving intimacy in one's life, and what a blessing that is as one gets older.

As a way of concluding this chapter on intimacy, I would like to share some reflections by a variety of people: The late Arsene Totoosis mentioned at a Men's Wellness conference, "Intimacy is the ultimate of being real." Thomas Moore adds this thought: "Without intimacy the soul goes starving, for the closeness provided by intimate relationships fulfils the soul's very nature."[24] And Paul J. Philibert contends that "God's agenda is transformation through intimacy, not moral self-improvement for respectability."[25]

Food for thought as we continue our journey into personal growth, human development and inner healing for especially the second half of life.

7

Being Mellow in a Bitter World

There are two inner spaces for grace
that I am learning to treasure.
One has to do with the tiny but eternal space
we make room for,
when we hold off, even for a split second, the negative –
even violent – reaction to a sudden hurt, allowing into our
souls a sliver of saving light. In that tiny oasis we recover
our almost-lost balance and center,
our precarious peace. It lasts the space of a breath –
but hides heaven.

—*Daniel O'Leary*

Being Old and Mellow

Fr. Robert recounts being stopped on the street one day by an elderly woman who asked him, "You are a priest, aren't you?" After he assured her he was, she went on to tell him, "I know too many old priests who are angry and bitter. I hope when you get older, you won't be like that. I hope you can be like me. I am an old woman, but I am mellow. I have forgiven everyone in my life who hurt me, and I have asked for forgiveness from everyone in my life whom I have hurt. I have been reconciled with everyone. I am mellow, and I am ready to die. I hope when you get to be an older priest, you can be mellow like me."

This incident underlines the need in our lives for forgiveness and reconciliation wherever it is needed and whenever it is possible. This challenge follows us into the last half of our lives and gains urgency as we grow older. As this elderly woman noted, it is indeed sad to see older persons who are bitter rather than mellow, who are still carrying a burden of anger and resentment.

Camellia came out of desperation one day to share her burden of loss, frustration and hurt. Her husband is valiantly battling cancer, which demands much of her time, and she is grieving the loss of four relatives, friends and family members over the past year. Her greatest struggle, however, is with her ninety-three-year-old mother, who is angry, vindictive, controlling, manipulative and in total denial of any shortcoming on her part. She is constantly putting down her sibling (Camellia's beloved aunt); whenever Camellia tries to change the subject or share her feelings, her mother begins to shame and berate her as an ungrateful, spoiled child. I shared her deep sadness at an elder who is not aging well, who chooses to berate instead of bless.

Letting Go of Our Story

The Returning to Spirit (RTS) process developed by Algonquin facilitator Mark Pizandawatc and Sr. Anne Thompson SSA addresses buried anger in a unique way.

Many people, when hurt, find themselves unable to forgive. Instead, they carry the hurt feelings, mull over them, vent them over and over again, or stuff them as deep within themselves as they can.

Worse, they tend to magnify that hurt into a story that keeps on getting bigger, darker and deeper as the years go by.

The image Pizandawatc uses is someone standing in a river of flowing water, looking downstream, scooping up buckets of stale water and throwing it over their shoulder to contaminate the oncoming water, so one never experiences any fresh water! The RTS process seeks to strip away all the accretions to expose the core wound needing to be addressed. Once the core wound is identified, the process leads us to the stage where we can dialogue with another person symbolizing that hurt, culminating in forgiveness and newfound freedom. What is surprising is how many religious participants – priests, brothers and sisters who are well on in age – have carried a spiritual burden of hurt and anger without being that aware of it, yet all the time being affected by its presence.

Our Original Wound or Core Grief

Regarding that "core wound," at one time the funeral homes in Saskatoon, Saskatchewan, offered an annual lecture series to caregivers on pertinent issues around death and dying. One speaker, a religious brother, spoke about an original wound or core grief almost everyone carries that is usually accompanied by alienation, lack of communication, isolation, division, bitterness and resentment. According to his experience, there are few families not struggling with this situation.

Dealing with Our Family of Origin

Melissa comes from a very rigid, dysfunctional family background. Her weak and submissive father swallows every ounce of hurt coming towards him from a dominating, unforgiving, controlling, pious mother who effectively manipulates her family, managing to subversively control everyone to the extent she can. Her older brother, favoured by her parents, rebelled in his own rude way and doesn't speak to her. She survived by being a totally obedient, quiet, good daughter, who in the end stuffed all her feelings and took up a career she did not like because her parents did not approve of her choice. To this day, her family has never forgiven her for moving out in her late twenties to get married.

What is ironic is that she lives in total denial of her dysfunctional background, idealizes her family, is afraid of the emotion of anger and is largely unaware that she is slowly, subtly trying to form her husband into her father, blaming his family for all their troubles, which is stressing him out. She is putting their marriage at risk by dragging into it the dysfunction from her family of origin. A sad element of this scenario is they are both religious persons, attending church every Sunday – an example of her faith not connecting with her life.

While this situation may be more extreme than others, it is probably safe to say elements of this story ring true for all too many other couples, families and relationships.

I feel sad and puzzled at how so often our faith does not make a difference in our lives. All the more so because Jesus has given us a way out. In a passage that is perhaps the least appreciated and least understood passage in the whole New Testament, Matthew 18:15-17, Jesus very simply teaches us how to forgive.

Forgiveness: A Biblical Model

Here is how it works in that passage. Whenever someone, even in the church, does something to hurt us, we should go to that person directly, alone, and let them know how we feel. It is as simple as that. Most translations read "Point out their fault," but I think if Matthew were writing today, with a greater knowledge of psychology, he would encourage us to share our hurt feelings with that person.

If they listen to us, we have won them back. If not, we are to take two or three others with us, to widen the circle. I have done that with sexual abuse victims as they confronted their abuser, to assure their safety and provide an objective witness. If the offender still doesn't listen, we can take it to the larger community. And finally, if they remain obstinate, Jesus tells us to treat them like a tax collector or gentile!

Now, what does that mean? I used to think it meant change the locks on our doors, shun them or get a peace bond. I know of one set of parents who actually did lock their son out of their house for their own safety. But that is not what is meant here. In the gospel of Matthew, who is the tax collector? Matthew himself. What Matthew is saying is to treat them like Jesus treated him – he was a tax collector gouging the poor, and Jesus forgave him and called Matthew to follow him. And in the gospel of Matthew, who are the gentiles? Us – we are the ones to whom Jesus sent his apostles to teach his commandments, which are to love God with our whole being, love others as we love ourselves, love one another as he has loved us, and above all, love our enemies, which in the end means to forgive them.

Just how radical a teaching this is surfaces a few lines later, when Peter reacts by asking how many times they should forgive

– as many as seven times? Seven being a perfect number, Peter was pretty sure that should cover it. To his shock, and perhaps dismay, Jesus replied, "Not seven times, but seventy-seven times." That combination of perfect numbers (three, four, seven and ten) equals seventy-seven, the most perfect number of all in the ancient Hebrew mentality. The only number more perfect would be seven hundred and seventy-seven (777) – the ultimate symbol of wholeness, infinity and perfection.

Within that same numerology, the number six is the weakest number of all because it never made it to seven. Sixty-six is an even weaker number, and six hundred and sixty-six (666) is the weakest number of all, symbolizing Satan. He is a weakling, already defeated, although he doesn't know it and is still causing havoc around the world, such as terrorism and acts of violence.

On that note, a mosaic on a tabernacle in St. Mary's Oblate Residence in Battleford, Saskatchewan, created by Fr. Al Hubenig OMI, beautifully illustrates this reality. A lamb holding a victorious processional cross, with blood pouring out of its chest, stands over a skeleton lying on the ground and wielding a sword. The message is clear – Jesus has won the victory, and even though Satan still does horrible evil, he is a 666 and defeated. He has already lost the war, even though the battle rages on.

So what Jesus is saying to Peter through the number seventy-seven is if he is going to follow Jesus and be his disciple, Peter can't just forgive once in a while. He must become like Jesus, who is forgiveness and never stops forgiving. Forgiveness must become part of Peter's DNA – it must ooze out of him. This same teaching applies to us. We must also become forgiveness – it must be part of our DNA if we are to follow Jesus and be his disciples.

So, for Jesus, to forgive is not optional – it is a commandment, how we can best love those who hurt us in any way. For some, it may seem like an impossible command. During a workshop I was conducting, one participant was visibly upset by this assertion. She finally told the group that not only was her brother murdered, but at the trial, the murderer showed no remorse and mocked the family's victim impact statement. She said forgiveness had been shoved down her throat all her life, but the closest she could come to it now was to ask God to forgive the murderer and leave it at that. Given situations such as hers, and given that the command to forgive is the core of the gospel and of our faith, we would do well to examine it more closely.

Our Choice of Options

Whenever hurt comes our way, we have options. According to psychologists, the two main options are fight or flight. If we are anger-based people, we will instinctively react in kind, fight back, get revenge, even the score. (This was the literal meaning of the "eye for an eye" teaching of Exodus 21:24, which was an attempt to limit violence; one should not inflict on an offender worse harm than was done to us.) On the other hand, if we are fear-based persons, we will flee in all kinds of ways – shunning, avoidance, silent treatment, or medicating our pain through some addictive behaviour.

There is also a third option a friend taught me – freezing. When her father, an alcoholic who had sexually abused her as a child, came home tipsy, she would freeze and try to become invisible. The danger here is our emotions can become frozen as well, morphing into a grey numbness that is hard to define. Recently, I have noticed some authors beginning to write about this option.

In this passage, Jesus is teaching us to transcend these options, to sink deeper roots of faith in God's love for us, to trust in him and his teaching more fully, to follow his example, and to practise a fourth option – forgiveness.

What Is Forgiveness?

> To forgive is to let go of anger and resentment, any desire for revenge or getting even, any attempt to fight, flee or freeze. It is to defy all logic and opt for the possibility of both forgiveness and reconciliation.

Forgiveness is a journey more than a destination, a process more than a program, a freeing up more than a closing down, a bold move into the unknown more than retreating behind protective walls. It is an offer of love, the only power that will last into eternity and break the cycle of violence in this world. Actually, it is a power that makes eternity present in this time and space (to err is human, to forgive is divine), and makes manifest more than anything else the very reign of God that Jesus came to inaugurate.

To forgive is to take in all the negative energy directed towards us, and rather than react in kind, to hold it, ponder it as Mary pondered these things in her heart, pray over it, vent the painful feelings if necessary, and humbly ask God, who is forgiveness, to do what we cannot do on our own – transform that dark energy into forgiveness, which is pure love.

Communicating with Love

This process is complete when we can give those dark emotions back to our abusers by communicating with love. That means letting go of the outcome and any expectation, because to communicate with expectation is already manipulation, and not love. That would be to try to change, or get something out of, the other person, and that is not pure love. Only pure love will set us free – the love Jesus demonstrated on the cross.

Communicating with love also means sharing our feelings and the impact the other's actions had on our life without any attempt to punish, exact revenge or get even. Then it is pure love, and I want to repeat: only pure love as forgiveness breaks the cycle of violence in our world.

Forgiveness as a Process

We have endless opportunities to practise this commandment of Jesus. Following the teaching of Jesus in Matthew 18, we can choose to go to anyone who has hurt us, ask them if we can share something personal with them, remind them of their hurtful behaviour, share with them our painful feelings and the impact their actions had on us, tell them we are trying to forgive them, and then let it go and give it to God. That is forgiveness, and it will set us free as well as give us new life.

Although it is not necessary to go to the hurtful person to forgive them from the heart, it is advisable to do so if at all possible. Why? Put simply, to practise Incarnational spirituality – to put flesh to our forgiveness in a way that makes it concrete for us, informs the abuser of the depth of hurt their actions caused us (of which they might not be aware), and above all, opens a door towards reconciliation. It is an invitation for them to apologize, a desired yet unlikely outcome, as most people, it seems, have no idea how to respond. This will be discussed in a later chapter.

Biblical Models of Forgiveness

When we forgive, we are just like Jesus on the cross: "Father, forgive them, for they do not know what they are doing" (Luke

23:34). When we act like God, we get to feel like God – peace, joy and a sense of freedom will fill our whole being. For sexual abuse victims especially, their innocence, dignity and self-worth return, for they are just like Jesus on the cross, and it doesn't get better than that.

Another biblical model is Mary, the mother of Jesus, at the foot of the cross. She was not screaming, attempting to stop the crucifixion, or claiming her son was innocent. No, she was a strong woman, standing at the foot of the cross, silently taking in all the dark, violent, negative energy of the crucifixion and pondering it, holding it, praying over it, forgiving those who were killing her son, and believing somehow that God, in God's own mysterious way, would turn it all to the good, which is just what God did, in the resurrection.

There are times when darkness must have its hour, and there is nothing we can do to stop some senseless violence from taking place. But we can, in faith, lessen some of the darkness, take it into ourselves and be like a water filter taking in dirty water and giving back only clean water. We do this through forgiveness. These are the groups of faithful who, at scenes of capital punishment, silently stand nearby keeping candlelight vigils, praying for both sides and in that way refusing to add to the dark energy of the world.

The Power of Forgiveness

Some years ago, Steve Hartman aired an episode as part of the series *Assignment: America* on CBS News that strikingly illustrated what genuine forgiveness looks like. On February 12, 1993, Mary Johnson's twenty-year-old son Laramiun Byrd was shot to death during an argument at a party by sixteen-year-old Oshea Israel. Laramiun was her only son. Mary was devastated and saw Oshea as an animal that had to be caged. He was sentenced to over seventeen years in prison.

As Mary's grieving process unfolded, she wondered as a devout Christian if there was some way, somehow, she would be able to forgive her son's killer. She began to visit him in Minnesota Stillwater State Prison, got to know him, and eventually forgave him from her heart. As she put it in the documentary, "Unforgiveness is like a cancer that eats a person from the inside out." Forgiveness was for her own well-being as much as it was for him. When Oshea was released, she invited him to move into her apartment building, and now he lives next door to her. Not only do they live close to each other – they are close. Mary treats him like the son she lost.

For his part, Oshea is trying to prove himself, to himself, and pay back Mary's mercy, working by day, attending college in the evenings, and speaking about forgiveness to large audiences everywhere. Johnson truly lived the teachings of Jesus.

From Surviving to Thriving

Here we return to Delores and her challenge to forgive the abusive resident of the seniors' home. At one point, she participated in a retreat where the story of Jesus washing the feet of Peter was presented with the help of biblical art by the late Fr. Sieger Köder. The painting portrayed Peter with one hand raised, resisting, and the other resting on Jesus' shoulder, accepting.

At the end of that session, Delores was in shock. When I asked if she was okay, she replied, "That's me! That's me!" She saw herself in the painting – as Peter. She knew she had to forgive the person who hurt her, but was afraid to. I invited her to stay with those thoughts and feelings in the safe environment of the retreat. The next morning, she shared with me that she had morphed overnight – now she was Jesus, knowing she had to wash that person's feet by trying to forgive her.

We discussed how God doesn't really want survivors, but "thrivers." Delores wanted to thrive, not just survive, and according to our faith, the best and really only way to thrive in this situation was to forgive that person. So, we worked on that challenge, using what Jesus teaches in Matthew 18:15. I suggested she write a letter to this person to communicate her hurt feelings with love as a way of trying to forgive her.

It took Delores two weeks to remember and relive the hurtful events, identify the hurt feelings, feel the feelings by staying with them, and not run away from them in any way. She was able to name, validate and honour those feelings and not stuff them anymore, which is actually emotional abuse, as she had done all her life. By doing so, she was loving herself, which is part of the Great Commandment Jesus gave us.

She then wrote a letter to the person who had wronged her, describing as accurately as she could and with as many details as she could remember all the hurtful incidents that had happened over the past few years as a reminder to this person. Delores poured out her emotions on paper with love – no desire for revenge, no attempt to get even, no name calling or desire to punish. Marriage Encounter teaches that love is a decision. For Delores, this is truly when love became a decision: a decision to try to forgive and not retaliate in kind. She ended her letter by saying she was trying to forgive this resident. It took faith, courage and inner strength to write the letter, and to overcome some trepidation and fear to give it to this person. She truly lived Jesus' command to love our enemies.

Significantly, this resident gave no indication whatsoever that she had received the letter. It was as if the letter had never been written, and the non-response was difficult for Delores to accept. She shared a lot of anger, frustration, sadness and disappointment with me over our next few sessions. I suggested that the non-response was this person's way of trying to retain some control over her, and the more her focus can be on her own growing relationship with Jesus, that need will become less. Delores was finally able to let go of any outcome and be at peace.

Fast-forwarding this story, there was no change of behaviour on the part of the other resident, which led to a second letter a year later, as a way to forgive her again. I had to marvel at the growth in patience Delores experienced over that year and gave thanks to God for the mature love she extended to this abusive person in her life by trying to forgive her.

Delores's growing desire for solitude and quiet was a sign of her maturing relationship with God. I affirmed the excellent work she was doing on her spiritual journey, especially around forgiveness. What was also very beautiful to see was the serenity, renewed zest for life and even joy Delores was experiencing as she entered her mid-eighties – she was truly becoming a wise elder, a Sophia who could now help others journey towards the same goal of serene forgiveness.

That opportunity to help others came rather quickly. Shortly after she had written the second letter, her nephew surprised her by coming to her for advice and support in dealing with anger towards someone in his life. Delores suggested to him the same process she had used: stay with the feelings, no blaming, no desire for revenge, express his feelings with love and let go of the outcome. After a few attempts at writing, her nephew produced a letter they both viewed as well written and ready to send. The letter had very positive results, as her nephew and the one who had offended him met, were reconciled and are now on good terms. This process was not only helpful to him but also to other members of his family, who were relieved and grateful that the painful issue was resolved.

Let's look at another example. Sam was involved one evening in a heated political conversation with Gus, an eighty-year-old man who was rigid and set in his ways. Sam left that encounter with mixed emotions that took him a while to sort out. In his busyness, he tried to put it all out of his mind, but in quieter moments nagging feelings hovered over him like wispy dark clouds. Eventually, knowing the importance of dealing with one's emotions, he allowed himself time and space to get in touch with his feelings. It dawned on him that he was feeling hurt, angry and judged at what Gus had said, as well as guilty and afraid because of how he must have hurt Gus in return.

Being a person of faith, Sam knew what he had to do – put into practice Matthew 18:15. He sat down, relived the incident and their conversation, and started writing. First, he asked Gus to let him know if he had said or done anything to hurt Gus's feelings – and if so, he wanted to apologize. Then Sam described the things Gus said and did that hurt him, and shared his feelings of hurt, anger and being judged. Sam ended the letter by saying he was trying to forgive Gus.

Sam hesitated to mail the letter, as he had never done anything like that to an older person before. However, trusting the process and the teachings of Jesus, he stamped and mailed the letter. A few months later, he happened to be in the retirement home where Gus lived, and met him in the lounge. Sam asked if he had received his letter a few months earlier. Gus replied that he had. When Sam asked if there was anything they needed to talk about,

Gus swept his hand angrily down in front of him, said brusquely, "It's all in the past," turned and walked away.

Sam was stunned and shocked at the anger in Gus's voice, in what he said about it all being in the past when it seemed to Sam it was very much in the present, and by the abrupt way Gus turned and walked away. Sam realized Gus was unable to apologize and did not know how to receive an apology. He felt sadness that the encounter ended the way it did, but more so for Gus, who at his advanced age was unable to handle this situation and move towards reconciliation. More importantly, Sam felt free and even some joy – he had lived his faith, had tried to forgive and be reconciled, and could now let this incident go. Sure, there was sadness at the lack of reconciliation, but he had done what he could and was free to move on.

Some years later, Gus died. Sam went to the funeral. He viewed the body at the back of the church, paid his respects, said a silent prayer, and touching Gus's cold hand, said silently, "Gus, now you understand." During the celebration, Sam felt sad that Gus missed out on experiencing reconciliation during his lifetime, but that emotion was overshadowed by the joy Sam felt at having at least done his best in trying to love Gus into new life.

This chapter on forgiveness began with an intriguing quote from Daniel O'Leary. I want to end with a variety of thoughts on forgiveness from other noteworthy persons:

Martin Luther King Jr. taught that "forgiveness is not an occasional act – it is a permanent attitude."[26] According to a quote attributed to Max Lucado, "Forgiveness is unlocking the door to set someone free and realizing you were the prisoner." And Richard Rohr claims, "forgiveness is simply the religious word for letting go."[27]

The last word, however, I would like to give to Sr. Joan Chittister OSB:

> To forgive is to be like God. God the Forgiver stands before us, beckoning us to holiness, showing us forgiveness as the way to wholeness: to mental health, to personal growth, to independence of emotions, to freedom of soul. Among Jesus' last words on the cross are words of forgiveness. Jesus – come to the fullness of humanity, the end time, the final moment – goes burned into our mind as a forgiver. Clearly, to be everything we can become, we must learn to forgive.[28]

8

The Art of an Apology

A stiff apology is a second insult ...
The injured party does not want to be compensated
because he has been wronged;
he wants to be healed because he has been hurt.

—G.K. Chesterton

Our Struggle to Apologize

I once accompanied an eighteen-year-old girl as she sought, by communicating with love, to forgive an eighty-year-old man who had sexually abused her when she was a child. That incident of abuse had a devastating impact on her life. Unable to share what had happened to her with anyone, her buried anger, shame and confusion led her to eventually medicate her pain with acting out, alcohol, drugs and sex. In the end, she lost her trust in men and is now in a same-sex union.

During our encounter, she cried her way through her letter. As she finished, she looked up and, with tears in her eyes, did as I had coached her – tried to understand him. She asked him why he had done that to her when she was eight years old – had something like that happened to him when he was young? Beautiful, I thought to myself – she is doing this perfectly.

He paused for a moment, then said flatly, "You really want to know? It's because of the way you were dressed." The children in that community used to go swimming in the lake; they would drop in to visit this older man on the way home, wearing their swimsuits, and that is when he molested her.

I could hardly believe my ears, and quickly interjected, "I feel angry, sad and disappointed when I hear you blaming her for something you did to her, whatever age she was." I turned to her and asked what she needed from him. She replied, "An apology."

I faced him and said, "She would like an apology." He paused for a moment, then said curtly, "Well, I'm sorry if I hurt you."

To me, that was not an apology. It was more an excuse, making it look accidental: certainly not taking in the gravity of his actions, but rather minimizing the impact they had on her. Realizing this was as far as we were going to get, we got up and left. I asked as soon as we got outside if she was okay and she replied, "Yes, at least I know he knows how I feel," so we continued home.

Believing this interaction was incomplete, I went to see the man a few days later and pleaded with him to do more, to at least write a short note of apology to affirm her integrity and lessen the pressure on her from many members of her community. They did not believe her when she opened up about this abuse and were blaming and revictimizing her for the loss of his services to the community. He waved his hand in front of him as if to dismiss the incident and exclaimed, "Oh, I took care of it in confession."

I felt both angry and sad at those words. To me, that was an abuse of a sacrament as a Catholic – using it to avoid taking responsibility for his actions. For her part, she dropped the charges against him, which was unfortunate, as he reoffended. What really saddened me is that this man, a churchgoing older man like the older person with whom I tried to be reconciled, seemed incapable of making a genuine apology, and missed an opportunity to be reconciled with the person he had abused. I went to see him years later, as I knew he was getting older and did not want him to die unreconciled, but he only got angry and told me to mind my own business. This is the bitterness our mellow elderly lady spoke about earlier, and it is truly tragic, especially for someone approaching his final days on earth.

Unfortunately, this type of bungled apology is all too common; indeed, in my experience, it is probably the norm. Very few people, it seems, have any idea how to apologize for the hurt they have caused others in a way leading to any possible reconciliation. Given that we are to be ambassadors of reconciliation (2 Corinthians 5:18-20) and being reconciled with others is an essential ingredient for both a life of wellness now and preparation for eternal life, this chapter will try to address this lacuna.

A Biblical Injunction

Two key passages in the gospels around reconciliation occur in Matthew. We have seen how Matthew 18:15 and following is all about the need to forgive. The flip side of that teaching is Matthew 5:23, which is all about an apology. In this passage Jesus states that if we are in church, have our gift at the altar, and realize someone has a grudge or resentment against us, we are to leave our gift at the altar and first go and seek to be reconciled: then we can go to church and bring our gift to the altar.

These are very strong words. I suspect if we took them literally, a good portion of any given congregation participating in Sunday morning worship would have to get up and leave to seek reconciliation. I know of one community where a mother and daughter go to communion in different lines so they won't have to interact. It makes one wonder if they have ever heard or read these words of Jesus. With such a firm, clear teaching, it is imperative that we examine it more closely.

Opening the Door to Reconciliation

As we have seen from the example above, making an apology is fearful for some, confusing for others, and resisted by many. Yet it can be a powerful initiative, opening the door to reconciliation – if it is done well and not stiffly, as Chesterton mentions in the opening quote. Let's go through what should constitute an apology step by step, and the reason why I chose to entitle this chapter "The Art of an Apology" will be evident.

Step 1: Obtain permission.

One can start by asking permission to share something personal with the other. This can do much to set a pleasant tone for the encounter.

Step 2: Remind the other person of your hurtful behaviour.

Ask if they remember the incident, and if not, remind them of it, describing your behaviour in as much detail as you can.

Step 3: Invite them to share their feelings.

This is a very important part of an apology. (One Indigenous woman told me she left the church for ten years after the Oblate Provincials in Canada issued an apology in 1991 for the legacy of the Indian residential schools, because no one had taken time to hear her story.) This step means being willing to be quiet, not react, listen and above all soak up the pain of the other person.

Just as we are starting to truly forgive someone who hurt us when we share our feelings with them by communicating with love, now the persons we have hurt are offered an opportunity to start forgiving us by sharing their hurt feelings with us.

Of course, they may not be capable of sharing or ready to share their feelings, and we have to be prepared for that. This is all about doing what we can to make things right, so the other person must be allowed total freedom to respond as they see fit. As in forgiving, we have to enter into this without expectation and be ready to let go of the outcome.

Step 4: Ask for forgiveness.

Now, after soaking up the painful feelings of the other, we can humbly ask if they can find it in their hearts to forgive us. Ideally, there should be no pressure or expectation. Some would even say that to ask for forgiveness is already putting pressure on the other. Again, we must leave them free to respond as they will.

Step 5: Make a declaration.

Algonquin facilitator Mark Pizandawatc taught the necessity of making a declaration during a training session for the Returning to Spirit process. When two trainees were late and no class member knew how to handle the situation, he simply turned to the two women and said, "Can I have your word that you will never do this again?" They gave him their word, and he went on with the class, but used that incident to teach us that "an apology without a declaration is almost meaningless."

I was struck by this teaching and wondered why it had never been presented to me so clearly before, in all my formation as a member of the clergy. A traditional Act of Contrition contains within it a firm resolve addressed to God to not sin again ("I firmly intend, with your help, to do penance, to sin no more, and to avoid whatever leads me to sin"), but there isn't a clear suggestion to make a declaration "never to act in that way again" to the person we have offended.

Bob somehow deeply offended a relative whom we will call Colleen during a conversation over the phone. Colleen called her mother and told her about the incident through her tears. Her mother called Bob immediately to let him know how hurt Colleen was. Bob wasn't clear just what he had said to so offend Colleen, but knew he could not argue with her feelings, so he called her back to apologize. She, however, was not ready to extend any forgiveness.

Desperate to resolve this painful situation, Bob drove to the city in another province where Colleen and her husband lived, took them out for supper and apologized again. He left that supper with the feeling his apology was still not accepted. That suspicion was confirmed at two family reunions over the next few years, as the husband especially was very distant and aloof with Bob.

Upon hearing this teaching about making a declaration, it struck Bob that perhaps this was something he could try. He called Colleen's husband and reminded him of the incident that was now years old, to which her husband said, "Yes, I have certainly been very cool towards you." Taking a deep breath, Bob said he would like to renew the apology, and added the declaration, "I want to give you my word I will try never to act that way again."

To his shock and pleasant surprise, the husband responded immediately, "Good – now that I have your word about this, I will certainly treat you more warmly." They started talking about a sport in which the husband was involved. They were reconciled. Bob has since visited Colleen and her husband, and the relationship is friendly. Bob is very grateful for this teaching on making a declaration that both completed his apology and brought about a renewed and highly valued relationship, which is the goal of a sincere apology.

Step 6: Ask how to make things right.

Steps eight and nine of the Twelve Step program teach this well. Step nine states, "Made direct amends to such people wherever possible, except when to do so would injure them or others." Having gone through all the previous five steps of the process described above, it is time to ask how we can make amends, to make things right again between the other person and ourselves. This step completes the reconciliation if the other person is willing to forgive.

Becoming One Again

The experience of Fr. Armand Nigro SJ with couples involved with the Vietnam war was enlightening with regard to this challenge of reconciliation. Nigro worked with veterans and their wives after the men returned home from the war. All the couples who tried to pretend nothing had happened and pick up where they left off broke up, he said. Only the couples who went through a process of reconciliation survived intact. I will outline the process I call "Becoming One Again" as he shared it with us:

Union – the relationship the couple had before the husband went off to war.

Separation – an invisible spiritual wall starts to build up between the spouses as soon as they are separated. They are already – in small ways at first, and in ever-growing ways – becoming strangers to each other.

Reunion – the husband comes back from the war and they are reunited, but the invisible spiritual wall is still there between them, even though they are physically in the same house and bed.

Reconciliation – each spouse had to trust the other completely and share their story, in as much detail as they could, taking as much time as was needed. There was more love in trusting the other with the truth than in withholding information out of fear of hurting or upsetting the other. The challenge for the other was to not react, just listen, and eventually forgive their spouse. This is truly where faith in God and each other, and love as a decision, comes into play.

Communion – if each partner was able to trust totally, empty themselves completely, share everything – the good, the bad and the ugly – have no secrets whatsoever, accept completely, forgive from the heart and let go of any resentment, then their relationship moved from union to communion – an even stronger relationship than they had at first.

This is what Jesus is referring to in the incident with the woman who washed his feet with her tears and dried them with her hair – a very sensuous scene that scandalized his Pharisee host. "Her sins, which were many, have been forgiven; hence she has shown great love" was Jesus' comment (Luke 7:36-50). The end result of "communion" is what can give couples the courage to go through this process of reconciliation. The more we mess up, the more honest we are, and the more we trust, the more we are forgiven and the more love we offer and receive. We can't lose. With God, everyone wins. God always turns everything to the good for those who love him.

Three Important Distinctions

This whole area of forgiving and apologizing is fraught with dangers and often blurred by confusion between these two similar but very distinct initiatives.

It is helpful to keep three clear distinctions in mind:

Forgiveness

Forgiveness is the process of letting go of anger and resentment, and any desire for revenge, punishment or getting even. Forgiveness is primarily for the one who has been hurt and does not depend on the response of the offender.

Pardon

Pardon is the process of letting go of any legal proceedings that could involve incarceration or some other form of punishment or retribution. One can forgive without having to pardon – in fact, it may be better not to pardon if there is any danger the person might reoffend.

Reconciliation

Reconciliation occurs when a relationship is renewed and even strengthened by forgiveness offered and an apology made that includes soaking up the person's pain, a request for forgiveness, a declaration never to offend again, and an offer to make amends.

While this is my own perspective on reconciliation, I am open to and do not want to exclude other viewpoints. Elder Maggie Hodgson claims the Indigenous have a cultural way of arriving at reconciliation based on visiting and offering gifts. I would invite a genuine respect and appreciation for all manner of reconciliation – whatever works best for the individual is paramount.

Some Stories of Reconciliation

Let's begin by looking back over the incident of the young woman trying to forgive her abuser earlier in this chapter. Having explored the various stages involved in crafting an appropriate apology, we can see now what was missing in this elder's response to her story and request.

In his first response, he actually blamed her for what he did to her and took no responsibility. In his second response, there was no real apology, no declaration to change, and no offer to make amends or make things right. The only thing he did do correctly was listen to her letter. She clung to that one redeeming factor. Unfortunately, there was no reconciliation, although she was able to forgive him, let it go and move on with her life. This supports the view that forgiveness is primarily for the victim who was hurt, and not the abuser.

I would like to balance this disappointing incident involving an older man with an amazing story of reconciliation involving an elderly couple I mentioned earlier, A.J. and Patricia, who gave me permission to share their story.

I had invited them to speak about Indigenous spirituality at a formation session for spiritual directors that was to cover Indigenous ministry, issues and spirituality. When A.J. started his talk, he spoke not about spirituality, but about what was on his heart at that moment (as Indigenous elders are wont to do), which was love and forgiveness. I felt concern and disappointment at first, but in the end, I am so grateful he did.

A.J. (he joked that those initials stood for "After Jesus!") shared his story about being a miserable alcoholic who mistreated his wife, Patricia, for years. He was an angry person, short-tempered, often drunk, combative, absent for long periods of time, gambled away much of their finances, and partied a lot. At one point, he felt so down on himself and useless, he wanted to take his own life. He would go for long walks, wondering why his wife was still with him.

Finally, unable to stand himself anymore, he came home one day and told his wife to sit down, because he was going to tell her who the man she married really was. He proceeded to share with her his whole life story – the good, the bad and the ugly, holding nothing back: everything he had done to hurt himself and others, as well as her. Her reaction was to get physically sick, vomit, fall silent and not talk to him for a week. He went for long walks, wondering if she would be there when he returned.

One day, after about a week of the silent treatment, he returned from one of his walks only to be told by her to sit down, because she wanted to tell him who the woman he married really was. She proceeded to tell him her whole story – the good, bad and ugly, holding nothing back. Now it was his turn to get angry, pull away and not talk to her for almost a week, as he continued to take long walks.

Then, mysteriously, something seemed to shift within and between them, and they found themselves building a sweat lodge together. After it was completed, they heated up rocks, brought in water, and had their own sweat together. That was it – they were reconciled, and A.J. claimed they have never talked about that episode in their lives since then. Now they are truly elders, King and Sophia, able to give workshops together. This was truly a cultural way of forgiving and apologizing to each other, of being reconciled, of living out both Matthew 18:15 and Matthew 5:23.

Another memorable incident of reconciliation took place in a cemetery. Velma asked me to accompany her to visit her mother's grave. I stood behind the headstone, in the role of her mother. Velma addressed her mother out loud, trying to forgive her mother for all the ways her mother had hurt her, and also apologized for all the ways she had acted out of anger and hurt her mother in turn. Then it was my turn to share what I thought her mother would have said in response. I felt awkward, yet deeply moved to be trusted in this way, and to help bring about reconciliation between Velma and her deceased mother.

Velma's life had been skewed by a man who raped her at the age of fourteen. After years of dysfunctional reaction, she went on a marvellous healing journey and arrived at the point where she wanted to try to forgive her rapist. Following the teachings of Matthew 18:15, she wrote a letter to her abuser and asked me to be with her as she met with him. Velma cried her way through her letter, communicating her feelings to him with love as a way of trying to forgive him. What happened then, totally unplanned and unexpected, blew me away – she apologized to him for the way she had treated him for forty years! Now that was amazing grace. I have since seen her dance with him at a social function and sit by him at a banquet.

That is forgiveness and an apology come full circle, and a sure sign Velma is living in the reign of God. Certainly, she has lived out in her life that comment of Chesterton's that began this chapter: she did not need compensation, she just wanted to heal because she had been hurt and had hurt others. As an addiction worker, she is helping her community to heal and serves as a model for us all.

9

From Stuck in Grief
to Good Grieving

> The greatest of all narcissistic wounds
> – not to have been loved just as one truly was –
> cannot heal without the work of mourning.
>
> —*Alice Miller*

A Common Ignorance

When I was still in formation as a young Oblate scholastic, I noticed a poster on a retreat house wall advertising a grief workshop. I remember wondering what that was all about, who would need such a workshop, and smugly thinking to myself, certainly not me.

Fortunately, it did not take long before a rude awakening knocked me out of my blasé attitude towards grief and grieving. In my first year of ministry in a small northern community, there was an urgent knock on my door one night. I opened it to find a group of excited children shouting, "Francis shot himself!" I ran to his small dwelling, arriving before the police, and was shocked to witness my first suicide, the sickening smell of death permeating the air. Shaken, I prayed for him as best I could, left after the police arrived, and tried to face the hard question – why?

That incident, I believe, kickstarted me into a journey of appreciating the need for all of us, but especially men, to deal with our losses and emotions around those losses, or those emotions will deal with us in very harsh, even brutal ways. Rohr expresses it well in this statement:

> Most men do not know they are really sad, and their lives are filled with unfinished hurt. They found ways to get rid of the pain before they really 'suffered' it and learned its good lessons. Many men think they are angry, but most male anger is really hidden sadness. To resolve this disconnect, almost all male initiation rites had to teach young men to weep.[29]

My background in Indigenous ministry resonates with this teaching that applies very much to Indigenous men whose traditional lifestyle of trapping, hunting and fishing has been taken away from them, leaving them especially vulnerable to sadness and being stuck in grief.

That incident of someone taking his own life, and all too many others similar to it over the years, suggests to me that I was not alone in my ignorance of the need to grieve our losses or remain emotionally crippled and at risk of acting out in dangerous ways. Thankfully, today many resources are available to help us deal with this challenge. This chapter will strive to be a small beacon of light along the way.

Being Stuck Can Be Deadly

There is a world of difference between being stuck in grief, and good grieving.

When for whatever reason (shock too great to handle, already overwhelmed with other emotions, a weak or misinformed faith, and so on), one is not able to grieve one's losses, a situation of "stuckness," an inability to move on with one's life, will be the unhappy result.

A young man whose father had abandoned the family and whose mother was an alcoholic took his life one day. A year later to the day, his younger brother took his own life. He was stuck in grief, did not have the resources to deal with his loss, and thought death was the only remedy. Ironically, only then did his mother hit bottom with her addiction, go for treatment and try to begin a new life for herself and the rest of her children.

As an aside, this mother was one of two women who came to visit me some years earlier, feeling guilty after they had fallen off the wagon and gotten drunk. There happened to be an AA meeting that evening, so I encouraged them both to attend. They refused, saying they were going to head south for a while, sober themselves up, and then they would start attending the meetings.

That was an early brush with blatant false pride, a deadly attitude that is the exact opposite of the humility needed to truly start to heal. This humility is the core of step one of AA – "Admitted I was powerless over alcohol, that my life was unmanageable." I cannot help but wonder if the woman's two sons might still be alive today had she come to that meeting.

A family came to see me one morning during a mission I was giving in their community. The parents were in agony, as their eldest son had taken his life seven months earlier. A downturn in the economy and a break-up with his girlfriend proved to be too much for him. The younger brother of the deceased, who came with them, was just as stuck in grief as the parents, because of his closeness to and love for his brother.

Emotions poured out of them as they shared their story – shock, anger, guilt, fear, shame, sadness and depression all mixed together in a grey shroud hovering over them since that fateful day. And now they were wondering – what could they, should they do, to try to deal with this trauma, to find some shred of hope that would help them go on living with any degree of light in their lives?

I listened attentively and tried to soak up their pain as much as I could. Fortunately, I had my laptop computer on the desk in front of me in the church foyer, on which I had saved a half-dozen articles on suicide written by Ron Rolheiser. He writes one such article a year and gets more reaction from that one article than any other he writes. For some people, he offers hope and meaning. Others remain skeptical, some think what he writes is too good to be true, and some accuse him of not taking the issue seriously enough.

I began sharing some of the articles with this family, grateful I had this resource on which to lean. Rolheiser sees suicide as emotional cancer, too powerful an enemy to overcome for some sensitive (gifted) persons, who often are trapped behind spiritual walls that no one can break through, try as they might with all the love they can muster. The biblical image Rolheiser uses is the appearance of Jesus to the disciples huddled in the upper room behind locked doors. Jesus comes through those locked doors and solid walls to disperse peace, joy and forgiveness, with no trace of anger or retribution. When all the love of family and friends cannot reach a loved one whose inner pain overcomes them, the love of Jesus can.

It was gratifying to hear the brother, especially, identify with what Rolheiser had written, and to witness the whole family begin to let go of some of the intense emotions they had been carrying, start to forgive themselves their imperfections, allow some hope for their son and brother's eternal destiny to enter into their hearts, and above all, take some small steps towards grieving and mourning his loss rather than staying stuck in grief.

Good Grieving

Viorst, in *Necessary Losses*, addresses all the losses in our lives, from our first breath to our last. Here is her conclusion:

> I've learned that in the course of our life we leave and are left and let go of much that we love. Losing is the price we pay for living. It is also the source of much of our growth and gain. Making our way from birth to death, we also have to make our way through the pain of giving up, and giving up some portion of what we cherish ... And in confronting the many losses that are brought by time and death, we become a mourning and adapting self, finding at every stage – until we draw our final breath – opportunities for creative transformations.[30]

Her book can be an invaluable resource for anyone dealing with loss. I would add just one thought to the above quote:

Losing is the price we pay for loving, as well as for living. The more we allow ourselves to love someone else, the greater the danger we may feel loss when that love must end. The saying "It is better to have loved and lost than never to have loved at all" applies here.

While being stuck in grief can be deadly, turning grief into grieving can be energizing and life-giving. That lesson came home to me during a four-day fast in which I participated one summer in onihcikiskwapiwin (Saddle Lake), Alberta. Our Oblate Task

Force on Indigenous ministry had organized a series of these fasts with the help of some elders. Every year that I was part of this fast, a new awareness would dawn on me.

One year, I was burdened by my resignation of a leadership position within the Oblates a year earlier. That action took away many interesting experiences and opportunities to serve that could have been mine, leaving me feeling sad. As mentioned earlier, I also feared I had lost the respect of my brother Oblates, adding grief to my sadness. Over breakfast one day, just before going out to fast, I overheard Maggie Hodgson, former director of Nechi Institute and Poundmaker Lodge in St. Albert, comment that eighty percent of the residents of the Poundmaker Lodge Treatment Centre for addictions were struggling with unresolved grief issues.

When an elder checked on me the second day into the fast and asked how I was doing, I responded I was doing well, but was wondering about that comment on "unresolved grief issues" lingering in my thoughts. "Stay with it," was his advice.

That afternoon, as I was about to pick sweetgrass, I noticed a log sizzling on the fire I had burning. Immediately, I thought with my scientific mind that this was a fresh green log. There was water in it, water expands when heated, and this water would have to come out somehow. The different-coloured rings and two termite holes in the end of the log made it look like a smiling face. While I was observing all this, sap started oozing out of one of the termite holes. Suddenly it hit me – this log is crying! The message to me was clear: Sylvain, you have to cry, to grieve.

Uncertain about how to do this, and certainly feeling uncomfortable with the idea, yet pushed into action by this "crying log," I wandered down the trail to where an old car sat abandoned. The windows were still intact; not wanting to disturb any of the other men who were fasting close by, I sat in the car and decided this was as good a place to cry as any, if I could.

I started to remember all the things that had not worked out in my life – the loss of my language and culture in the hospital as a French-speaking child at the age of five; the lack of involvement in sports and intramural activities as a day student at a high school focused on boarders; no recreational activities with my father while growing up; a year out of university because I was confused about what to study; resigning as president of the university college students' association because I still had no major in my third year; and finally, resigning as provincial of our Oblate province due to my workaholic burnout that I had no way of dealing with and did not understand.

I had stuffed all these memories, and the emotions linked to them, for years. Now, in that car, they all landed on me at once. I started to cry. I hit the steering wheel, but hurt my hands, so I started to hit the car seat. The old car filled with so much dust, I had to get out to breathe. But to my surprise, I felt a sudden surge of energy as I emerged from that car. It was like a vacuum cleaner had cleaned me out, and I could tackle the world. With a start, I suddenly realized I had grieved! I had done it – it had happened. I had turned being stuck in the grief I was only dimly aware of into good grieving. I was set free to move on in a new way.

A Spirituality of Grieving

A good definition of spirituality is it is all about letting go. This process of grieving is similar to the process of forgiving, as both involve precisely this spirituality of letting go. Whereas in forgiveness one must let go of anger, resentment, bitterness and any desire to punish or exact revenge, in grieving one must let go of sadness, self-pity, sorrow, depression, inertia and any tendency to isolate.

Every hurt contains within it a loss of some kind. Something has changed that will never be recovered and must be grieved. Hurt un-grieved will often come back as hardness and depression. From my own experience and that of others, here are some steps to grieving along with some brief comments on each step.

1. Remember the events and relive the experiences

> Our faith is based on remembering; addiction is based on trying to forget and medicating the pain.

Grieving begins by remembering the incidents of loss and trying to relive those incidents to the degree we can, realizing that the only way through the pain is through the pain.

2. Identify and name our losses

Sorting out and naming our losses will help us to sort out and identify the emotions tied in with those losses. The key to mental wellness can be helpful here: face our losses, accept our losses and deal with our losses.

3. Feel and stay with the emotions, especially sadness and self-pity

No one likes to feel these painful emotions, so the natural temptation is to avoid them. However, the healing of these emotions lies in our ability to feel and experience them. Healing happens when these painful emotions are transformed into their opposite.

4. Express the emotions positively

Grief shared is grief diminished. Often people act out of their emotions instead of simply sharing them. Venting is a positive action if the feelings are intense. Writing out the feelings and sharing them with a trusted other is perhaps the best way to express them and turn grief into grieving.

5. Mourn and grieve the losses

The need to do this may seem self-evident on the surface, but I find that for myself, some action was needed to bring the tears to the surface. Men especially struggle with this challenge. I remember listening to an audiotape in which the speaker mentioned that many men are afraid if they start to cry, they won't be able to stop.

It is important to be aware of the difference between grieving and mourning. Grieving is more private, dealing with our emotions around loss by ourselves, as they hit us at different times and with different intensity. Mourning is more public and done with others. Wakes, funerals and rituals celebrated with others provide a safe environment that not only offers support, but also touches emotions lying deep within us and facilitates the expression of those emotions. A word spoken, a poem recited, a prayer prayed, a song sung can all slip deep within us and elicit emotions we perhaps did not even know were there.

6. Give yourself permission to cry

Crying is an important part of the grieving process. We can give ourselves permission to cry as much as we need to.

Sometimes, well-meaning people are too quick to offer solace that can actually hinder or block the grieving process.

As the eldest child, Rose was often told not to cry, to be strong for her siblings. At her mother's funeral, she took those words seriously and did not allow herself to cry. When she received a letter from her family at a retreat for youth years later and heard me say to the group, "It's okay to cry," she began to wail. As she put it later, it was like something broke inside of her. Finally, she was giving herself permission to cry, and she started to grieve.

7. Take a workshop on grieving

Over the years, I have moved from wondering what a workshop on grieving was about to being firmly convinced of their value. Dr. Jane Simington of Edmonton offers workshops on Trauma Recovery and Grief Support under the umbrella *Taking Flight International*. She uses symbols, music, rituals and right-brain activity to reach places deep within our being where grief may be stored that words alone could never reach.

8. Say the words "It's gone, it's gone."

Denial is a natural defense mechanism that helps us survive, but God wants us to thrive, not merely survive.

Saying out loud and to ourselves, "It's gone, it's gone," is a way of breaking through any denial still holding us back, and a way of opening the door to good grieving.

A Biblical Model of Grieving

An incident in the Bible that speaks eloquently of grieving is the appearance of Jesus to Mary Magdalene (John 20:1, 11-18). Mary had gone to the tomb, inconsolable, to grieve her loss. After Peter and John had entered the tomb, seen the linen cloths and departed, Mary remained there, weeping. When Jesus called her by name, she recognized him, cried out, "*Rabbouni!*" (which means teacher), ran to Jesus and very naturally wanted to give him a hug.

Jesus then spoke these significant words to Mary: "Do not hold on to me, because I have not yet ascended to the Father." What he was teaching her is yes, he was back, but she could not have him back as he was before. He had risen, not just to earthly life again, but to a new kind of life, eternal life, the life he wanted to share with her, the other disciples, and us. The Jesus of history is now the Christ of faith.

So, Jesus was teaching her and the other disciples to grieve and mourn his loss, let him go and let him ascend to the Father. Then he would be able to send her, and them, his Spirit to be with them in a new way, and they would not miss him anymore. And that is what he did, at Pentecost.

Luke, in the Acts of the Apostles, puts it this way: "After his suffering he presented himself alive to them by many convincing proofs, appearing to them during forty days and speaking about the kingdom of God" (Acts 1:3). I am convinced he was also teaching them to grieve and mourn his loss so they would be open to receive the Spirit when it came. The number forty need not be taken literally. Biblically, it symbolizes the time it takes to bring something to completion, fullness, wholeness. Jesus succeeded in convincing them, for in Luke 24:52, we hear that the disciples "returned to Jerusalem with great joy." They had successfully grieved and mourned his loss, and were now open to the new life he offered them.

To conclude this chapter on grieving, I would like to share a few quotes that in their own way can touch our souls:

An anonymous person said, "Our bodies hold the tears our eyes have never shed." Joyce Rupp, in her book *Praying Our Goodbyes,* offers this spiritual insight: "If Calvary is the deepest goodbye anyone has ever known, then the resurrection is the greatest hello anyone has ever proclaimed."[31] And Elder Maggie Hodgson teaches, "Tears are the rainbow of the soul."

10

A Spirituality of Aging Graciously

The problem is not old people getting angry,
but angry people getting old.

—Eugene LaVerdiere

It is not enough to add years to life;
one must also add life to years.

—John F. Kennedy

A Matter of Perspective

To my surprise, I began to look forward to each visit.

Although the pace of my life and ministry did not lend itself to visiting the ailing and elderly, I made a point of visiting Auntie Thérèse, my late mother's sister and one of the two remaining aunts in our family, as often as I could. At the age of ninety-two, widowed, frail, losing her sight and her hearing, and finding it difficult to walk, she was now in a seniors' lodge.

She never really complained – just wondered why she was still alive when her husband and square-dancing partner, Uncle

Louis, had passed away years earlier – and said how she longed to be with him. What surprised me was the joy I felt just being with her, enjoying the sound of her voice, her gentle touch, the sharing of memories with her, and especially knowing she was, day in and day out, thinking of her nephews and nieces, and praying for us all.

I found myself pleading with her not to leave us, not yet – we needed her. She still had a purpose to accomplish – we needed her patience, her faith, her acceptance, her love and caring, and above all her prayers. And at a deeper level, I realized I needed her – to help slow me down, to pull me out of my too fast and too full pace of life – to come to her room that was an oasis of peace and quiet, to learn to just "be" for a few moments.

Just to be in her presence was a calming and soothing balm for my overstimulated and overloaded mind and body. In a way I did not fully understand (nor did I need to), I sensed that in visiting her I was touching the deepest values of life, even glimpsing in a dim way the edge of eternity. I knew each visit might be the last time I would see her and enjoy her warmth and love. We both knew the end, death, was lurking just around the corner, but it was not an enemy. It was just a friend who would bring to completion and closure the beautiful, wonderful life lived to the full on a farm, raising a family with all the joy and pain, successes and failures, suffering and consolation that entailed.

When she finally did breathe her last, we were able to celebrate a life and a death become, in the words of St. Mother Teresa of Calcutta, "something beautiful for God."

Visiting my mother was in some ways similar, and yet different. She had Alzheimer's disease, and we lost her to the disease seven years before she died. My mother was an educator as well as a farm wife, a gentle, gracious, elegant yet unpretentious woman who ensured we had music lessons and a good education, and full of faith in God. We went to mass every Sunday in the family car to our parish eight miles away on gravel roads, and prayed the rosary at home every May and October. The closest Mother ever came to swearing was to exclaim, "Jésus, Marie, Joseph" in her French accent when things weren't going well.

Our grieving began when we realized she was losing her cognitive ability and no longer recognized us. Eventually, we could not communicate with her at all. I would sit silently by her bed and shed tears, regretting all the things I would have liked to share with her or ask her, but no longer could. Finally, I began to visit at mealtimes when I could feed her, the only way to elicit a response from her.

Then, similar to how it would be with my aunt, I began to realize I needed my mother and her inability to communicate – to force me to slow down, be more patient, learn to just be, appreciate the infinite worth of the human person created in the image and likeness of God, love her for who she was and not for what she could do, and reflect on the meaning of life and death. Even though she couldn't do anything, she still had a profound, almost mystical purpose – to teach me the deepest of life's lessons.

Our society today, in its lack of faith and spiritual depth, offers us a limited and narrow perspective on aging, illness and suffering – trying to convince us that it has no meaning or purpose, and should be avoided at all costs.

Hopefully, the sharing of my experience of journeying through old age and illness with my aunt and mother holds forth a more hopeful and positive view. The rest of this chapter will attempt to lay a foundation for this faith perspective.

The Two Halves of Life

There are many ways of viewing our pilgrim progress through the years of our lives. Dividing our lives into two halves is probably the most common and efficient way of dealing with this challenge, so let's start with this basic division. As mentioned in the introduction, I will be basing myself mostly on Richard Rohr, who has spoken and written extensively on this topic.

According to Rohr, various models of human development suggest there are two major tasks for each human life. "The mystics of all the great religions, along with classic literature like Homer's *Odyssey*, intuited that life was a journey involving completion of a first half and transition to a second half, sometimes called 'a further journey.'"[32]

It has been said one cannot live the second half of life with the same rules by which one has lived the first half. They simply won't work anymore, so something has to change. We need a new set of rules by which to negotiate the challenge of aging. An important task of Christianity is to help people move from the first to the second half of life within these new rules.

The first task is to build a strong "container" or identity; the second is to discover, identify and enjoy the contents the container was meant to hold. We all try to do the task life first hands us: establishing an identity, a home, relationships, friends, community, security, and building a proper platform for our life.

At some point, we begin to sense that there has to be more to life than we are experiencing. We start questioning the meaning of life, a signal that we are moving into the second half, that in many ways will feel like being "in a dark wood," as Dante put it in *The Divine Comedy.*[33]

As we enter this dark wood, what guided us in the first half of life begins to shift. One of those pillars may be our religious faith. Religion in the second half of life becomes more mystical than moral. It is less about trying to be perfect, and more about seeking to become more passionate; less about keeping laws and more about living the law of love.

Rohr states that the danger of staying in the first half of life is we start to make it our "private salvation project." Often, it takes a crisis of some kind – failure, an illness, a challenging relationship or accident – to get us to let go and move on into the pain of further growth and facing the fearful unknown.

As a number three on the Enneagram,[34] my greatest need is to succeed and my greatest fear is failure. And wouldn't you know it, into failure is exactly where I was led, to knock me off the self-sufficient and comfortable path I was carving out for myself. Two resignations, one as provincial of my local Oblate province and two decades later as a bishop governing a northern archdiocese, both due largely to my workaholic pace of life, took me where I dreaded to go: the bottom rather than the top.

This was the only way, it seems, I would realize I had become a "human doing" rather than a "human being" and learn the hard lessons of life: self-worth comes from being rather than doing, God's love cannot be earned, ask for help, be humble, face my fears, love myself for who I am rather than for what I can do, I am not the messiah, and life is ultimately about relating and not producing.

In this second half of life, we develop a both/and manner of thinking, as well as a win/win mentality. We become more aware of our own defects and shortcomings, and more able to "weep" over our own phoniness and hypocrisy. We can begin to let go of the need especially for power and control in our lives and become more able to "let go, let be and let grow."[35] If we stay stuck in our certitudes and attitudes of superiority, we will stay in the first half forever, and never fall into that Great Mystery.

A grade 11 student had given me a card in the first years of my ministry in which she had written these words: "May the Lord shine his light into the dark areas of your life." Taken aback by this card from such a young person, I mentally pushed that prayer far back into my mind. Now I realize how prophetic the card was, for that was precisely what was happening. I needed to, as Rohr expresses so well, "fall upwards."

> Ironically, many religious people never allow themselves to fall, while many sinners fall and rise again.

Jean Vanier touches on this reality with his claim that people with an intellectual disability not only understand the message of the gospel more quickly, they often live it at a deeper level than most people. They know what it means to trust in God, to give him their hearts, to love him and be loved by him.[36]

Vanier would agree with Rohr that life becomes more simple and unified as we come to accept ourselves as we are. This brings with it a certain peace and serenity. In the second half, we try to influence events, work for change, quietly persuade, change our own attitude, pray, and forgive instead of attacking things head on.

Life is also more spacious in the second half of life, as we are more and more able to face reality, accept reality and deal with reality, a key to mental health and wellness mentioned earlier.

There is a sense we are all in this together, and are more willing to just be part of the flow of life rather than assert ourselves to stand out. As Rohr puts it, life is more *participatory* than assertive, and there is no need for strong or further self-definition. God has taken care of all that, much better than we ever expected. The brightness comes from within now, and it is usually more than enough.

Very relevant and crucial for workaholics like me, we have moved to an utterly new kind of doing that flows almost organically, quietly, and by osmosis. Our actions are less compulsive. We do what we are called to do, and then try to let go of the consequences. We usually cannot do that very well when we are young, which alludes to the seasons of our lives that we will discuss next. Now we aid and influence people simply by being who we are. Human integrity probably influences and moves people from potency to action more than anything else.

Rohr states:

> We don't move towards the second half of life until we've gone through the first half and the transition period.

The sequence, therefore, is order-disorder-reorder. And we *must* go through disorder or there is no reorder! St. Paul calls this "the foolishness of the cross" (see 1 Corinthians 1:18-25). This sequence also connects with the Positive Disintegration theory of Dr. Dabrowski, mentioned earlier.

Rohr would claim that until we can trust the downward process, the Great Mystery cannot fully overtake us. It's largely a matter of timing. Some of us put it off until the last hour of life. But the sooner we can do it, the better. Almost all spirituality teaches us the secret of "dying before we die."

If we can face our mortality and let go of this small self sooner rather than later, we'll experience heaven here and now. After all, we do pray daily, "thy kingdom come." We'll begin to experience the freedom of the children of God. So, the sooner we can trust and allow the precipitating event, the sooner we will understand the resurrected life, and we'll live by a life not our own. According to Rohr, that's the whole gospel in a nutshell. None of us can engineer it; we simply wait and watch and surrender to it. Rohr's writings are a valuable resource for anyone wanting to study this theme more deeply.

The Stages of Discipleship

Whereas Rohr speaks and writes about the two halves of life, Rolheiser prefers to speak of three phases of life, based on St. John of the Cross, albeit with different terminology. Rolheiser also casts these stages into the framework of discipleship: Essential Discipleship, Generative Discipleship, and Radical Discipleship.

The stage of Essential Discipleship, which John of the Cross calls the Dark Night of the Senses, begins after puberty. From our birth to puberty, our lives are more or less together, barring some serious dysfunction or trauma. Puberty is designed to drive us out of the home, to find and build a home of our own until we can come back home. Essential Discipleship is the struggle to get our lives together, to establish ourselves in the world. The questions in this stage include these: Who will love me? Where will I live? What career path should I take? Is God calling me to a particular vocation? Most popular songs are focused on this stage of our lives. Our struggle here is with the energy of youthfulness.

The second stage is Generative Discipleship, or the stage of Proficiency for John of the Cross. In this phase of generativity, we are now established and settled, with a career or vocation, family, community involvement, and so on. The struggle here is to give our lives away – to use our God-given gifts and talents to make the world a better place. The questions in this stage include these: How can I be a better person, parent, minister? How can I be more altruistic, generous, creative in fulfilling my purpose in life? This stage will take up most of our adult years.

Eventually, however, there is a shift – perhaps a mid-life crisis, a questioning of "Is this all there is? Could there be more to life than what I am experiencing at the moment?" There may be some career disappointment, some unaccomplished goals, a restlessness creeping back in. This subtle shift moves us into the direction of the last stage of our lives, the stage most relevant to us as we age, Radical Discipleship, which John of the Cross calls the Dark Night of the Spirit. We will return to this stage in the next chapter within the context of human suffering.

A Biblical Basis for Personal Growth

Closely related to the view of the two halves of life, yet also leading us into a more complex, three-part division, is the teaching of Walter Brueggemann on three major parts of the Hebrew Scriptures: the Torah, the Prophets, and the Wisdom literature. Again, I rely on Rohr's insights into this scriptural perspective.[37]

The Torah, or the first five books of the Bible, corresponds to the first half of life. This is the period in which the people of Israel were given their identity through law, tradition, structure, certitude, group ritual, clarity, and chosenness. That is the "safe container" our family of origin is supposed to provide for us by meeting our need to be loved, belong and be valued.

The second major section of the Hebrew Scriptures is called the Prophets. This introduces the necessary suffering, "stumbling stones," and failures that initiate us into the second half of life.

> Without failure, suffering and shadowboxing, most people (and most of religion) never move beyond narcissism and tribal thinking. But healthy self-criticism helps us realize we are not that good, and neither is our group.

It begins to break down either/or, dualistic thinking as we realize all things are *both* good *and* bad. This makes all idolatry, and all delusions that go with it, impossible.

Living this second stage well allows us to move to the third section of the Hebrew Scriptures: Wisdom Literature (many of the Psalms, Ecclesiastes, the Song of Songs, and the Book of Job). Here we discover the language of mystery and paradox. This is full immersion into the second half of life. We are strong enough now to hold together contradictions, even in ourselves, as well as in others. And we can do so with compassion, forgiveness, patience and tolerance. We realize our chosenness is for the sake of letting others know they are chosen, too. We have moved from the Torah's exclusivity and "separation as holiness" to inclusivity and allowing everything to belong.

The Seasons of Our Lives

Closely linked to Brueggemann's teaching on the three stages of biblical development is Rolheiser's teaching on the seasons of our lives. The invitations that Jesus extends to us in the gospels come to us at different seasons of our lives and apply to our lives accordingly. Some are intended for the first part, some for the middle and some for the last part, and it is important we make that distinction.

This wisdom flows from a homily Rolheiser gave on the importance of "being rather than doing," of "acceptance rather than achieving." He was making the point we need to take our self-image from who we are and not from what we do, or we will always pursue achieving something. He based himself on trustworthy sources such as Henri Nouwen, Thomas Merton and St. Mother Teresa of Calcutta, and therefore felt confident in presenting his material.

However, after the homily, a young man disagreed with him. He pointed out that the sources Rolheiser used were all high achievers. It is easy, but rather ironic, he said, for them to teach that one's worth is not measured by what one does or produces, because their achievement is all behind them. Nouwen wrote over sixty books, Merton helped recover mysticism in the West, and Mother Teresa is a saint. It sounded hollow to this young man to say we don't have to achieve anything to feel good about ourselves after having achieved our goals. This young man asked, what about him – an ordinary, unknown, mediocre person who hasn't really achieved anything in life and struggles as a result with low self-worth, lack of confidence and low self-esteem?

That challenge helped bring home to Rolheiser that biblical teachings, rather than being taken literally, should be interpreted according to the seasons of our lives. It is important to distinguish between the first half and the second half of life, because the biblical invitations are specific to these seasons and not indiscriminate.

One example would be the passage about Martha and Mary of Bethany, in which Martha chides Jesus for not caring that Mary was leaving her to do all the work herself. Jesus in turn gently chides Martha, claiming that Mary has chosen the better part (Luke 10:38-42). This passage is geared to those of us entering the second half of life, inviting us to be more reflective and contemplative, to slow down and spend more time being rather than doing.

On the other hand, the parable of the talents (Matthew 25:14-30) speaks to a person in the first half of life, during which time one has to be occupied with activity, with asserting oneself, with establishing an identity, career, home and family, and so on.

Rohr and Rolheiser share a common approach to the scriptures. I would encourage reading their writings, as they provide a framework of personal growth and human development for interpreting scripture and applying biblical teachings to our lives.

The Stages of Hindu Anthropology

During a Marriage Encounter weekend at a remote retreat centre some years ago, I noticed a book on Eastern spirituality in the library. What caught my eye was a section on Hindu anthropology that seemed relevant to this phenomenon of aging graciously, especially the last two stages of "Forest dweller" and "Sannyasin."

Sannyasin is a Sanskrit word describing someone who has reached the life stage of a *sannyasa*, or "renouncement of material possessions." Sannyasa (*saṃnyāsa*) is the life stage of renunciation within the Hindu philosophy of four age-based life stages known as *ashramas*, with the first three being Brahmacharys (bachelor student), Grihastha (householder) and Vanaprasstha (forest dweller, retired).[38] Rolheiser adds a preliminary stage, that of a child.

Sannyasa is traditionally conceptualized for men or women in the later years of their life. It is a form of asceticism that is marked by renunciation of material desires and prejudices, is represented by a state of disinterest and detachment from material life, is concerned with understanding one's inner life, and has the purpose of spending one's life in a peaceful, love-inspired simple spiritual life. They now live only to perfect their understanding of the spiritual world.

I know little of Eastern mysticism or spirituality, but these four roles of Student, Householder, Forest Dweller and Sannyasin seem to resonate with the two halves of life that Rohr posits, the three stages of discipleship taught by Rolheiser, and the role of King and Sophia of male and female spirituality.

The role of Forest Dweller is that of someone arriving at the end of their active generativity stage and entering into the second half of life. This would involve slowing down, giving up some active work or ministry and entering into a more reflective mode. It is a time to look back over one's life, move beyond knowledge accumulated from outside sources and arrive at a certain wisdom derived from one's own experiences. It might mean doing more reading, finding a spiritual director, doing some therapy, dealing with unfinished business in relationships, forgiving some people, apologizing to others, and going on an inner journey of healing one's shadow side.

The goal of this Forest Dweller process would be to arrive at one's own version of a Sannyasin, a wise older person, needing to do less, able to "just be" much more easily, ready to share their wisdom and help others go through the stages of their lives, wherever they find themselves. Aware that people are living longer and we do not have an adequate spirituality for our wisdom years, Rolheiser and the staff of the Oblate School of Theology have developed a two-year course designed to help participants enter into this stage of "Forest Dwelling."

Living in the Kingdom

One of the first things a newly appointed bishop must do is decide on a motto that will in some way capture and express the essence of his episcopacy. I have always been intrigued, fascinated and motivated by the fact that Jesus came to inaugurate the reign of God here on earth. I sometimes wondered why the kingdom of God did not seem to be preached that often, since it was the topic Jesus spoke about the most. And consciously or perhaps even unconsciously, all my ministry as a priest and now bishop has been trying to help build up the reign of God here and now.

As a result, it did not take long for me to choose a motto with the help of an older Oblate. It is from Luke 17:21 (*Regnum Dei Intra Vos* – The Kingdom of God is among You). This is the only passage in the New Testament where Jesus doesn't just say the kingdom is near or a person is not far from the kingdom – he states that the kingdom of God is a present reality.

The theological term for that teaching is "realized eschatology," coined by theologian C.H. Dodd, who taught that we should understand Jesus' message "the kingdom of God is at hand" with an emphasis on the kingdom's actual presence. In other words, the kingdom of God is already present, but not fully realized.

That present reality – living in the kingdom of God here and now – should intensify as we grow older and seek to experience that kingdom more fully.

Living Our Purgatory Now

Part of living both our radical discipleship and within the kingdom of God is the invitation to live our purgatory now, before we die. The notion of purgatory, properly understood, is one of the Church's most consoling and encouraging doctrines. Rolheiser has two very pertinent definitions of purgatory – "the pain of entering heaven" and a "letting go of the things of the earth." It is not a place we go to but a process of healing, reconciliation and transformation transcending the boundaries of physical death.

Purgatory is the invitation to face our shadow, seek forgiveness for our wrongdoing, admit and experience healing of our defects of character, let go of our addictions and seek reconciliation. We cannot drag any unfinished business into heaven – it doesn't belong there and cannot enter. It all has to be purged, refined, completed and transformed into love, especially through forgiving, apologizing and making amends. I sometimes tell those who are doing steps four to nine of the Twelve Step program (moral inventory, admission of one's wrongdoing, healing of negative attitudes and making amends) that they are living their purgatory now, and living it well, through the pain of working these steps.

I experienced purgatory in my relationship with my father when I wrote a letter to him eleven years after he died to share all my feelings about the way he raised us – feelings I had never shared with him when he was alive.

When a counsellor asked me if it felt more like an adult-to-adult relationship now that I had shared that letter with him by reading it out loud, I realized that was it! I was no longer a child and he a big daddy – we were friends, as I had shared my feelings with him in a very intimate way.

Then I had the amazing thought that I was helping my father enter heaven. If I was healing in my relationship with my father here on earth because of this letter, then perhaps he was healing in his relationship with me. The relationship with my father had come full circle: that was when I believe I received the spirit of my father to be with me in a new way.

This is the task of the second half of life, and of Radical Discipleship – to live our purgatory before we die, so we can live within the reign of God now. When the time for our physical death comes, we will be ready, and simply slip through that "thin place" of Celtic spirituality into the arms of a loving God who is waiting to share with us the fullness of God's love and life.

Accepting the Reality of Aging

A biblically wise person will let go of any denial and accept the reality of aging. Rosanne had to leave an abusive marriage, is now retired and on her own, a vibrant and joyful person. When she was approaching retirement and old age, she made the decision to not only accept but also look forward to that stage of her life. Because she had always been busy, working and raising a family (and dealing with an abusive husband), she resolved that one of the things she was going to do was rest and sleep as much as she wanted to and felt she needed to. She now sleeps two or three times a day and feels absolutely no guilt in doing so. She is practising the virtue of acceptance.

Facing Our Fears

John had been sent to a therapeutic centre to deal with a major depression in his life. He did not want to go and resisted the program once there, fearful of venturing into the unknown. His group attended a Eucharist on Christmas Day, during which he was unsettled by an unusual homily. The young African priest started recounting a story of lions hunting in Africa. John wondered what this story had to do with Christmas.

The priest related how an old lion with no teeth, who could only roar and not hurt a flea, would place himself on one side of a savannah, while the younger lions waited on the other side. When a group of impalas came along, the old lion would rear up on its haunches and roar. The frightened impalas would bound away from it right into the jaws of the waiting pack of lions. The priest ended his homily with the moral of the story. "Face your fears. They may be painful, but they won't harm you." With a start, John realized this homily was meant for him. His resistance left him; he began to participate in the program and started to heal.

Fear is one of the most common emotions people carry and the one holding many back from the change, healing and transformation that could be theirs. Jesus told us hundreds of times in the gospels not to be afraid. We need to take him at his word, find the courage to face our fears, overcome them and move forward into growth and healing.

Having a Ministry of Prayer

Making prayer and praying for others into a ministry is another way to add purpose and meaning, especially to the stage of Radical Discipleship. I would suggest that a goal in our diminishment might be to become more proficient in the practice of centering prayer and Lectio Divina, mentioned earlier, with its four stages of Lectio, Meditatio, Oratio and Contemplatio.

Ovide lost his wife years ago, which probably had an impact on his aging process. He can do little, is bent over and uses a walker inside the house. What gives him meaning and purpose is the ministry of prayer. People call him and ask him to pray for them or for some particular intention, and he takes that seriously. So that his prayer won't be interrupted, he sometimes even calls some of his children whom he suspects might be about to visit him to let them know that for the next hour he will be praying!

Insights into Aging

As I was completing the writing of this book, Ron Rolheiser happened to offer a retreat at the Oblate School of Theology in San Antonio entitled "Insane for the Light: Spirituality for Our Wisdom Years". Given that the topic fit the theme of this book like a glove, I joined a small contingent of Canadians who journeyed down to Texas to attend this retreat. My purpose was to glean what I could to add to this book.

As usual, the experience was rich beyond measure and impossible to compress into a few pages of a book. However, the material presented during this retreat will make up much of the content of a book Rolheiser will be publishing under that same title, so I would encourage the reader to read it when it is available. It completes a trilogy: a first book on Essential Discipleship (*The Holy Longing*), a second on Generative Discipleship, or Proficiency (*Sacred Fire*), and this latest on Radical Discipleship, giving our deaths away.

In his presentations, Rolheiser covered aging from biblical, anthropological and mystical perspectives. I would like to offer here a glimpse of some of the anthropological dynamics of aging that he shared with us, within the conviction that the intent of God, through nature, is for aging to bring us to wisdom by conscription.

A main source of this wisdom is James Hillman, a brilliant philosopher and Jungian analyst whose book *The Force of Character*, while a secular work, is considered one of the best books on soul. A key question is why God would design a process that involves the body starting to break down just when we reach our mental prime. Hillman's answer makes sense: the best wines have to be aged in cracked barrels. As the body breaks down, it matures the soul and forces it into wisdom and the realm of the spirit.

It takes the body years to break down, a process that starts usually around age thirty-five, when we are in our prime. This slow slide has an intentionality, aging us into wisdom, whether we want to or not. If we don't do it, it will be done to us. Aging is written into our DNA and has an important role – to bring us to wisdom and initiate us into a new way of life.

Rolheiser points out that with rare exceptions, such as St. Thérèse of Lisieux, there are no child prodigies in the area of wisdom, as there are in other fields such as the arts, music and sports. Wisdom is a seniors' game that comes only with aging and aging well.

> The value of elders can be compared to a rock in a river forcing the water to flow around it, adding character to the river. While success and achievement may bring glory to a family, it is aging and disabilities that bring the family character and depth. Our society has less character when we isolate our elders.

Hillman spells out the many ways the body breaks down and why. The body starts to sag because we have been carrying the weight of the world on our shoulders. We start waking up at night to keep vigil and deal with issues we are too busy to address during the day. As the body becomes less attractive, our sexuality takes on a new, richer modality, such as a grandparent blessing a child – this is the full bloom of sexuality. Our senses become dull, but more soulful. Heart problems may reveal the reality of troubled hearts from past hurtful behaviour. A tendency to push away children flows from the need to do inner work, and we begin to see essences rather than details – all part of God's grand design to bring us to deeper wisdom.

Germaine Greer and her book *The Change*, written for women about menopause, is another source of wisdom for aging. She points out that younger women are valued by society for their biology, a value lost after menopause. The need then is for women to grieve that loss and move towards the status of Sophia, a wisdom figure, and to be valued for that quality. Biology brings us to the place where we must look towards the value of wisdom. Among the Indigenous peoples, the role of elder can be the best phase of one's life.

Rolheiser presents Swiss psychologist Alice Miller and her book *Drama of the Gifted Child* as another source of wisdom on aging. For her, the gifted child is the sensitive child who wants to please, help and do good, which could be most of us. However, a lifetime of pleasing tends to bite us back when it is not rewarded, appreciated or reciprocated. Feelings of anger, envy and being cheated or treated unjustly surge to the fore, and our sensitivity begins to collapse. For Miller, at this pivotal point of life, the second half of life brings the spiritual task of grieving life's shortcomings and forgiving life's hurts.

With a sadness we all shared, Rolheiser informed us that Kathleen Dowling Singh, who had been invited to present during this retreat, had died of cancer. Her ministry as a hospice worker led her to write three books on living, aging and dying. Singh stresses that aging and dying are calibrated to bring us into the realm of spirit, to become as we were in our infancy, luminous and without ego. She teaches that we undergo four major spirit-soul contractions as we grow, leading us to our conscious awareness, including the formation of our shadow and walling off what frightens us. Aging reverses the process, takes us back through these separations, breaks down our shadow and leads us to face our dark side and deal with it.

The whole process of aging is designed to break down all the veils we have constructed, mellow us out and ready us for death. Interestingly, Singh adds three stages to Elisabeth Kübler-Ross's model: despair, surrender (which is deeper than Ross's acceptance) and, at the last minute, ecstasy. This process can be initiated by profound contemplative prayer, but few find that path. Still, we can take solace in the fact that aging is a preparation for something new rather than just the end of life as it was.

While this longer chapter is a blending of views and reflections on aging from many sources, I hope it will provide some direction for further study and action for those who may want to pursue some of the diverse paths mentioned.

11

Giving Our Deaths away as Gift

When one finds it his destiny to suffer, he will have to
accept that suffering as his task; the single unique task.
He will have to acknowledge the fact that even in suffering
he is unique and alone in the universe. No one can
elieve him of the suffering or suffer in his place. His unique
opportunity lies in the way in which he bears his burden.

—*Victor Frankl*

Touching a Sensitive Chord

A pastor in a parish I was visiting asked if I could preside at the morning liturgy. Looking over the first reading, I was struck by a line St. Paul addressed to the young bishop Timothy: "Join with me in suffering for the gospel, relying on the power of God" (2 Timothy 1:8). The congregation tended to be somewhat elderly; knowing the recent emphasis on medical assistance in dying, or physician-assisted suicide, I decided to be bold and speak on that issue under the title "Radical Discipleship and Redemptive Suffering." I was touched that for some days after, members of the congregation commented on that homily.

One person in particular remains in my memory. In the sacristy the next day, he quietly informed me he had been diagnosed with Parkinson's disease, and emotionally shared his fear of where that might take him. At the same time, he expressed gratitude for the homily the day before. It had given him encouragement and strength to move forward with less fear.

As Victor Frankl mentions in the above quote, suffering at some time or other will be our destiny. It does not help that our society today has lost any sense of purpose or meaning in suffering, leading not only to a lack of support for anyone whose situation includes suffering, but actually making it almost politically incorrect to speak of suffering in a positive light. For example, a psychologist in Ottawa wrote in *Maclean's* magazine in 2017, "We used to think the enemy is death. Now we know it is suffering."

This present-day mentality that sees no value whatsoever to suffering, wants to eliminate it at all costs, can only see it in negative terms and maintains that helping people end their own life is a form of compassion lends urgency to a discussion of the role suffering can and should play in our lives, especially as we age and approach the end of our time here on earth.

The Stage of Radical Discipleship

A most helpful prism through which one can meaningfully explore the whole area of suffering is the notion of Christian discipleship, and especially the last stage of Radical Discipleship, explained earlier.

> The struggle in this stage is to give our deaths away, very much as we gave our lives away earlier.

Home is where we start from; we then build our own home, but we don't die there – we have to go to another stage that becomes the journey of leaving this planet, and our final homecoming.

The ultimate paradigm of Radical Discipleship is Jesus. We commonly speak of Jesus giving his life and his death for us, but these are two distinct movements we are invited to live out. The gospels are divided into two clear parts – his public ministry, from the time he is announced by John the Baptist to his agony in the Garden of Gethsemane; and his passion, from the time he is arrested to his death on the cross.

From the time Jesus was arrested in the garden to his death on the cross the next day, he hardly did anything – everything was done to him. He was betrayed, arrested, led away, abandoned, tried, abused, ridiculed, denied, humiliated, probably sexually abused,[39] scorned, slapped in the face, spit upon, flogged, forced to carry a wooden beam, and finally crucified, a Roman form of capital punishment designed to inflict the maximum pain and humiliation on the victim.

As Rolheiser explains, Jesus became passive – a patient placed in palliative care who is dying. In all of this suffering, he did and said little – a few sentences to Pilate and the high priests, and the "seven last words" of our faith tradition. Everything was done to him. While this final stage of his life is called his passion, the more accurate meaning of that word, coming from the Latin *passio*, is "being done unto," his passivity.

In his activity, Jesus gave his life for us; in his passivity, he gave his death for us. Significantly, in those last eighteen or so hours of his life, we believe he did more to redeem the world than during all his active ministry of teaching, healing, and even raising the dead.

What is critical is how Jesus went through this *passio* – without bitterness or resentment. There was only love, compassion and forgiveness for his executioners: "Father, forgive them, for they do not know what they are doing" (Luke 23:34). He promised paradise to a thief, cared for his mother, and entrusted John and the church to her (John 19:26-27). Jesus also resisted the last temptation to use his divine power in a selfish way to avoid this suffering and come down from the cross.

After his resurrection, every appearance of Jesus to his disciples, who had betrayed, denied and abandoned him, was an experience of forgiveness. There was no trace of bitterness or resentment, just peace, forgiveness and joy – especially in the upper room (John 20:19-23) and by the Sea of Tiberias (John 21:15-19). The value of Jesus, powerless, broken and dying on the cross, is a great mystery. That Jesus did the most when he could do the least is a divine paradox.

Blood and water flowed from Jesus' side as he hung upon the cross. The temptation for those of the Catholic faith is to conclude that this symbolizes the sacraments of baptism and Eucharist. That is a legitimate claim, but there is a deeper level of meaning involved here. That blood and water symbolize the divine, eternal life Jesus wants to share with us here and now, within the kingdom he came to inaugurate. And because the birth of a child into this world involves the breaking of water, it is also a symbol of birthing new life, the new creation that John the evangelist emphasizes was brought into being by the resurrection of Jesus from the dead (John 20:1, 19).

A Spirituality of Radical Discipleship and Redemptive Suffering

Barring an accident that might cut our life short, as we age, Radical Discipleship will come to us in the form of illness or some other factor in our life over which we have no control. Essentially, we cease to be able to function normally on our own and begin to need help to do even basic things.

Those of us who claim to be followers of Jesus are invited to faithfully and freely appropriate all of this to ourselves. We are to take up our cross and follow him (Luke 9:23), to accept any suffering that comes our way, any inconvenience we may face, any obstacle that troubles us, the same way Jesus did, without bitterness or resentment.

That acceptance is the key to the messianic secret, the mystery of the cross, and the kingdom of God. If we can accept some suffering without bitterness or resentment, our suffering is connected to the suffering of Jesus and takes on profound meaning and purpose. It becomes redemptive, as we share in the suffering of Christ by which he redeemed the world.

This flies in the face of all logic and reason, touching as it does the mystery of suffering in the Bible. St. Paul articulates it this way: "I am now rejoicing in my sufferings for your sake, and in my flesh I am completing what is lacking in Christ's afflictions for the sake of his body, that is, the church" (Colossians 1:24).

Here, St. Paul is trying to explain what cannot be explained, to articulate what cannot be articulated – it is something to be believed and experienced. And we do experience it, for when we act like God, we get to feel like God. When we can and choose to live out Radical Discipleship with faith through a redemptive suffering that is able to forgive and accept, then we are just like Jesus on the cross, and it doesn't get any better than that.

A key to understanding how this can be lies in the last few words of that passage: "for the sake of his body, that is, the church." In St. John's version of the Pentecost event (the same day as the resurrection), Jesus breathes on the disciples, bestows the Holy Spirit on them, sends them out as the Father had sent him, and tells them, "If you forgive the sins of any, they are forgiven them; if you retain the sins of any, they are retained" (John 20:22-23).

With these words Jesus is saying that whatever they loose on earth is loosed in heaven, and whatever they bind on earth is bound in heaven. This is astounding, and the ultimate fulfillment of the Incarnation – that Jesus gives to his Body, the Church here on earth, the power to help build up, or hold back, the reign of God here and now. The sacrifice of Jesus is sufficient, but he has in a mysterious way made us participants in that sacrifice, so our sacrifice and suffering matter. In the same way, Jesus seemed to accomplish nothing on the cross from a practical and utilitarian point of view, yet in reality he accomplished our salvation.

So too the bedridden victim of some disease or old age who seems to have nothing to offer can join his or her sufferings to Jesus and, in this mysterious exchange of love, do great and wonderful things for others.

This is a mystery that our society simply does not understand at all. With its lack of faith and inability to appreciate suffering, society will constantly try to convince us to take the easy way out, to avoid suffering, to shun pain, ignoring as it does so any question of morality or conscience at all stages of life. Unfortunately, the harsh reality of this attempt to avoid suffering is often blurred by euphemisms such as "death with dignity" and disguised as a false compassion that can trick many faithful of goodwill to think these actions are morally permissible. For example, it is sad to see support in the media for a person who, fearing she may not be mentally competent to make the decision for physician-assisted suicide when her health deteriorates, chooses to end her life prematurely while she can still make that decision.

> When suffering loses its profound meaning and is seen as having no purpose at all, then of course the next logical step is to try to eliminate all inconvenience and suffering.

At one end of the spectrum, it will suggest abortion to avoid the inconvenience of having a child. In saying this, I want to acknowledge that there are many and often complicated reasons why a woman would choose to have an abortion. Some may become pregnant because of youthful indiscretion and panic at dreams dashed by an unplanned child; some may be pressured into this drastic action by others. I want to respect and not judge any person. I just want to make the point that our society will all too often claim only one way out of this dilemma – that which avoids suffering.

At the other end of the spectrum, society now holds up the ideal of helping people take their own lives to avoid the inevitable suffering of illness and old age. I once gave a presentation on the topic of Radical Discipleship and Redemptive Suffering at a seniors' residence. An elderly woman came up to me after the presentation to tell me she had considered putting her name on the list of those who wanted medical assistance in dying. However, after hearing the presentation, and learning that any suffering coming her way in the process of aging and illness can have profound meaning and spiritual purpose, she changed her mind. I felt affirmed in what I was presenting, and also joy at the positive, mature decision for life she had made.

It takes a deep faith to make the decision to accept suffering. In a powerful online reflection on Orthopraxy, Rohr brings faith and suffering together:

> I believe that, in the end, there are really only two 'cauldrons of transformation': great love and great suffering. And they are indeed cauldrons, big stew pots of warming, boiling, mixing, and flavoring! Our lives of contemplation are a gradual, chosen, and eventual free fall into both of these cauldrons. There is no softer or more honest way to say it. Love and suffering are indeed the ordinary paths of transformation, and contemplative prayer is the best way to sustain the fruits of great love and great suffering over the long haul and into deep time. Otherwise you invariably narrow down again into business as usual.[40]

This Spirituality Lived Out

Living out this spirituality of Radical Discipleship and redemptive suffering will probably be the greatest challenge most of us will ever face in our lives. For that reason, I would like to share with you the stories of some who have done so in an admirable way we could emulate.

Robert is typical of the struggle to give our deaths away. He was an active, honest, successful businessman who raised a large family. He was very involved in his community, giving much of his time to serving many civic organizations, and very charitable with his wealth. At the age of sixty-two, he was diagnosed with cancer and found himself dying in a hospital. He shared with a friend that he knew he was dying and could accept it. What he found very difficult to accept was that he had always been in charge, helping others, but now could do almost nothing and felt useless. He had moved from activity to passivity. For decades he had given his life away; now he had to learn to give his death away. Finally, he was able to ask for help. Anytime we are helpless and powerless, we are entering into passivity and Radical Discipleship. Theologian Teilhard de Chardin teaches that we need to sanctify the world through both our activity and our "passivities."[41]

Rolheiser's sister, a member of a religious congregation, was a dynamic person full of life and zest. She loved being dean of students at an all-girls' high school, loved being a religious sister, and became the heart of the family after both their parents died. One day she collapsed and was diagnosed with cancer. She was bedbound from that day on, and could do almost nothing for herself other than use the phone. Yet she kept her love for others alive, was gracious and patient, never complained and lived for nine months before the cancer claimed her life.

Perhaps nine months, the time it takes to gestate new life into the world, is not a coincidence. The family would agree that she did more in those nine months to influence and inspire them and others than in all her years of ministry, because of her unwavering faith, profound life of prayer, humble acceptance of her illness and constant caring for others. She lived her Radical Discipleship and redemptive suffering well.

My older brother Louis, during a trip to Toronto, suddenly began to communicate with slurred speech, was taken to a nearby hospital, went into a coma and had to be operated on for a brain tumour that proved to be malignant cancer. That event began a four-year struggle to survive, with its share of ups and downs, hopes and disappointments. My sister-in-law, Judy, took a leave of absence from work to look after him at home. The children and grandchildren came from across the country to visit as often as they could. I tried to spend as much time with him as my schedule allowed.

What struck me most about my brother during his long illness was his faith, patience, gratitude and graciousness (which he must have inherited from our mother). I was profoundly moved to receive his humble confession at his bedside a week after his operation in Toronto. He was always saying, "Thank you, Jesus," for everything, even after he lost his sight and until he could no longer speak. Apparently, he even thanked a nurse for a suppository she had given him! We suspect the last sense to go was his hearing, so we continued talking to him until the end. I will never forget seeing him reaching upwards at times, towards something, or someone. Deeply touched, I could not help but wonder what or who he was seeing in his blindness.

Louis died around eight in the morning in my sister-in-law's arms, as she had prayed he would. I am convinced that his life of love and his long experience of redemptive suffering made him such a radical disciple that he simply, silently slipped through the veil of that sacred "thin place" into the arms of his creator and loving God.

At the evening prayer service for him, everyone was given Easter tapers to hold up high while we listened to one of his favourite hymns. Deacon Bob Williston, whose music Judy had come to love, came to sing at the funeral. It was truly a faith-filled celebration of Louis's wonderful life and inspiring death in a church filled with family, friends, neighbours and acquaintances.

Blood and water were flowing from his side as we bid him farewell. We went away sad at our loss but energized and inspired to live as he had lived, and to die as he had died. Tributes to him poured in from all directions – to his honesty, his faith, his caring, his gentleness, his integrity. Some said they were better persons because of the way he lived and died. Both his life and his death were a blessing to all who knew him.

Living and Dying as a Blessing to All

How do we give our deaths away? The same way Jesus did. Blood and water can and should flow from our casket at our funeral if we have lived and died in a way that our life and our death are an optimal blessing to all who know us.

We may have been to funerals of someone who lived an unfortunate, self-centred life and died sadly, and then gone away from that funeral with the energy drained out of us. We have also attended funerals of someone who lived well, giving their life away, and who died well, giving their death away as a blessing to all who knew them, as my brother did. We depart from these funerals sad that we have lost a loved one, but also energized and inspired, refreshed and invigorated, motivated to both live and die as that person did. That is the mystery of Radical Discipleship and redemptive suffering.

What kind of funeral do we want to have? The choice is really ours. Victor Frankl puts it well in the quote at the beginning of this chapter, reminding us that no one can relieve us of suffering or suffer in our place. Our unique opportunity lies in the way we bear our burden.

Our challenge, and the challenge of our faith, is to live our Generative Discipleship well by giving our lives away, using our gifts and talents to make the world a better place, and then living our Radical Discipleship well through redemptive suffering by giving our deaths away, so that both our life and our death will be a maximum blessing to all who know us.

We began this chapter with wisdom from Victor Frankl. I would like to close it with wisdom from other sources:

Recovering alcoholics are well acquainted with suffering. An issue of *Grapevine*, the Alcoholics Anonymous newsletter, offers us this thought which provides an opposite view from the psychologist quoted earlier:

> Suffering is no longer a menace to be evaded at any cost. When it does come, no matter how grievously, we realize that it too has its purpose. It is our great teacher because it reveals our defects and so pushes us forward into the paths of progress. The pain of drinking did just this for us. And so can any other pain.[42]

I prefer to trust the experience of those in recovery rather than a merely academic view when it comes to handling pain and suffering in our lives.

Rohr offers another view on suffering in his online comments on Franciscan spirituality:

> If suffering is 'whenever we are not in control', then you see why some form of suffering is absolutely necessary to teach us how to live beyond the illusion of control and to give that control back to God. Then we become usable instruments, because we can share our power with God's power" (Romans 8:28).

And finally, a cryptic quote from Meister Eckhart to close this chapter: "Suffering is the swiftest steed to bring us to perfection."[43]

12

The Stages of Our Lives: A Mystical View

To lose the earth you know, for greater knowing;
To lose the life you have, for greater living;
To leave the friends you loved, for greater loving;
To find a land more kind than home, more large than earth.

—Thomas Wolfe

As noted earlier, aging can be viewed from biblical, anthropological and mystical perspectives. I think it appropriate to present a mystical perspective in this last chapter because in many ways, it encompasses and frames all that has been written about aging in this book. Based largely on the material Rolheiser has been presenting in retreats and lectures, this chapter can serve as a preview and taste of his next book, mentioned earlier.

The person best suited for this reflection is St. John of the Cross, perhaps the greatest structural mystic in the West. A Carmelite monk, he was also a systematic theologian with a doctorate in theology and philosophy. It is rather amazing that John of the Cross developed this schema five hundred years ago, without the benefit of contemporary psychology. For John, we make our way through six distinct stages of life that Rolheiser filters through the perspectives of prayer, love and service.[44]

Stage One: Pre-Conversion

In this early stage, youth have an unhealthy indifference towards life, a take-it-or-leave-it attitude. The basic motivation is a pleasure principle – life is all about oneself. There is an unhealthy complacency, a lack of commitment, a certain smugness and a need to look cool. These young people may be nice, but lack depth and character. Prayer is superficial, relationships are casual and service is barely on the horizon.

Stage Two: Conversion

Falling in love is the key characteristic of this stage. Life for the person changes overnight. There is a loss of indifference and an initial transformation of motivation from a self-centred to an unselfish principle. One becomes obsessed with what one has fallen in love with, and a new energy fuels the personality like never before. A spiritual experience of meeting Jesus, meeting the person of one's dreams, or an encounter with the poor for the first time suddenly opens up a whole new vista on life.

Stage Three: First Fervour

This can be compared to a honeymoon and is what John of the Cross calls the Active Night of the Senses. There is usually a high level of passion and excess in all areas, along with unabashed public display. There is boundless energy – nothing is too much for those in this stage. They have found love, Jesus, the poor. Discursive ability explodes – they can talk endlessly about the object of their love, and in this stage, men can even talk about their feelings. There is a desire for heroism and uniqueness, and a loss of balance that is not a problem – it feels wonderful. There is a sense that life is full and this is enough.

What is happening in this stage, at a deeper level, is that one is mainlining archetypal energy, Godly energy, real energy that is a taste of ultimate reality. The object of one's attention carries the archetypal energy of God. One is more in love with the energy of being in love than with the person, or Jesus, or the poor. Things are happening, but mostly on the surface. This is a powerful stage, but it won't last. Honeymoons are not meant to last – we come home from honeymoons to the reality of daily life.

Stage Four: Waning of First Fervour

This is the stage of disillusionment and what John calls the Passive Night of the Senses. It marks the death of the honeymoon. Disillusionment is not a bad word – it just means what one was experiencing before had an element of illusion within it. One moves from tasting the archetypal to seeing the real, as "experiencing the experience" loses its lustre and begins to dry up. One now begins to see the other as he or she really is, and not as a god or goddess. Boredom sets in, there is a loss of discursive abilities, and the struggle to adjust to reality begins. During this stage, there can be a growth in genuine solicitousness, a healthy anxiety (a positive worry about birthing the kingdom), a genuine concern for each other, for Jesus and the poor.

For St. John of the Cross, this is a critical time, because as Rolheiser puts it, the devil parks right here, at the door. Unfortunately, at this stage many succumb to the temptation to give up, to leave, to lose hope. The loved one is far from perfect, prayer becomes more of a challenge, and one finds the poor have many of the same faults as the rich. The danger is to think one has "done their thing" and can now give it up. This is where, as the poet Robert Frost wrote, one can take the road less travelled by, and it will make all the difference.

Stage Five: Proficiency

This is the stage Rolheiser calls Generative Discipleship. One makes the decision to continue with one's commitments. We choose to love, to pray, to serve, not because it feels good or for what we get out of it, but because it is the right thing to do. This stage can last for decades.

As we move into this stage, there will usually be a first phase of dryness, of having to make oneself perform, of daily making the decision to continue on the path one has chosen. However, eventually, we arrive at the second phase where the dryness turns into a certain ease, a sense of being at home. This is a move into a greater maturity and fruitfulness. Deep personal realities and characteristics start to develop under the surface, unlike the first stages.

One of Rolheiser's relatives shared an experience illustrating this sense of ease: Imagine an office where the younger staff are discussing the exciting things they plan to do on a weekend – sports events, trips, going to a bar, plays, and so on. When an older staff member is asked about his plans, he almost apologetically admits that he and his wife will make some popcorn and stay at home to watch a movie. A young secretary responds by admitting that all their planning is in the hope of someday being able to do just that – stay at home with a loved one and watch a movie.

Or imagine an elder mother in a nursing home with two daughters – one living in the Northwest Territories who visits once a year, and the other living nearby who comes to visit her mother five times a week. A visit from the daughter in the Northwest Territories once a year is certainly more dynamic, emotional and exciting, but who has the deeper relationship with the mother? The daughter who visits regularly. Sure, their conversation may be more mundane, because the deep conversations have already taken place. But visiting a mother in a nursing home every day allows the relationship to quietly and even imperceptibly grow into greater intimacy. In this case, presence becomes more important than words. Even falling asleep can be a communing of love and commitment.

Sometimes there isn't another stage – we may die first, perhaps because of an accident, in a stage of later generativity, giving our life away to make the world a better place. However, for St. John of the Cross, there is a final stage.

Stage Six: The Dark Night of the Spirit

This stage corresponds to Rolheiser's Radical Discipleship, and the notion discussed earlier of living our purgatory now. We enter this stage by choice, or by accident – an illness or some loss of control in our lives. According to St. John of the Cross, a first phase of this stage necessitates sufficient fidelity and maturity that builds up strength for a more radical setting out.

A second phase entails a radical decision based on the gospel, one that will seem to many as going against common sense and even being irrational. The biblical model for this phase is the story of Abraham and Sarah who, in their old age, are asked by God to leave the familiar and set out into the unknown; when they arrive, they will have their first child. Rolheiser claims that at this phase, it is healthy to be a radical fundamentalist and "roll our dice on the gospel."

Those who do enter into this stage will probably experience dryness in prayer, great turmoil and sharp doubt, even within a certain dark security. They may feel awful and experience a bitterness bordering on despair, but if they stay with it, they will enter the fourth phase, which John of the Cross calls the living flame or ecstasy. God will break through with occasional bursts of ecstasy – perhaps the same ecstasy that Singh writes about in her book. Mingled with that ecstasy will be a longing for consummation and even death. This only happens if the situation is absolutely radical, with no possibility of return.

In the first half of our lives, we struggle with the world, pleasure, sex, the devil, restlessness, the things of this world – what John of the Cross calls the Dark Night of the Senses. In the second half, there is a shift – we no longer struggle with the devil, we struggle with God, with doing God's will more fully, and hope God wins. This is what John of the Cross calls the Dark Night of the Spirit.

A biblical character illustrating this stage is the elder son in the story of the Loving Father and Two Lost Sons in Luke 15. The younger son is struggling with the energy of youth, lust, pleasure, sex – the Dark Night of the Senses. The elder son, on the other hand, is struggling with his father – there is great tension between them. He obviously has to deal with some deep, dark issues in his life – painful emotions of anger, bitterness, jealousy, being overlooked, and even deeper negative attitudes of unforgiveness, judging his brother, stubborn self-righteousness, false pride and lack of respect for his father – the Dark Night of the Spirit.

We are left wondering if the elder son was able to negotiate this most challenging stage of life, for the parable ends with him outside the banquet. This abrupt ending perhaps underlines the importance of putting energy, as we move into our twilight years, not only into living our generativity well, but also negotiating as best we can our own Dark Night of the Spirit as it comes to us.

It is interesting to view other ways of looking at the stages of our lives within the light of these mystical insights of St. John of the Cross.

In the end, one can say it is all about coming home – first of all, leaving home to establish one's own home, then leaving that home to arrive back home again for the last time and for all time.

Afterword:
Heaven Before We Die

A French-Canadian preacher, when asked the secret of his success, shared a simple formula: First, I tell the people what I'm going to tell them, then I tell them, and then I tell them what I told them!

Along that same line, I would like to sum up this book with some pertinent suggestions for ongoing growth:

Make your second half of life a healing journey,
find a soulmate,
learn to forgive,
be humble and willing to apologize,
seek to be reconciled,
mourn and grieve your losses,
practise contemplative prayer,
find a spiritual director,
live the Great Commandment,
walk around the Medicine Wheel with others,
face your fears, and
accept aging yet strive to be generative as long as you can.

And here is a final quote:

There are three ways to get to heaven without dying: to live fully in the present moment, since in heaven there is no time limit; to allow everything in life to move you and fill you with love, since the measure of love given and received is the only thing we get to take with us in death; and to give away those things that make for treasures in heaven like forgiveness, comfort, blessings, faith, hope and love.[45]

Hopefully, the reflections making up this book have provided insights into a practical spirituality for growing old with zeal, love and intimacy. May they not only help us get to heaven without dying, but also guide us into living in the kingdom of God here and now, through all the stages of our life.

Epilogue

The righteous flourish like the palm tree,
and grow like a cedar in Lebanon.
They are planted in the house of the Lord;
they flourish in the courts of our God.
In old age they still produce fruit;
they are always green and full of sap,
showing that the Lord is upright;
he is my rock,
and there is no unrighteousness in him.

Psalm 92:12-15

Acknowledgements

There is a saying, "It takes a village to raise a child." I find that applies also to writing a book – there are many people who, directly or indirectly, have had a spiritual or literary influence on these pages and to whom I owe a debt of gratitude.

Thank you to close friends Sr. Judy Scheffler SSND, Wendy Lickacz, Chris Carney and Dan Friedt for their overall comments and encouragement.

I am grateful for my spiritual directors over the years, especially Archbishop emeritus Adam Exner OMI for kickstarting my healing journey, Fr. Leo Engele OMI for helping to sustain it, Sr. Teresita Kambeitz OSU for helping me negotiate a crisis, Fr. Tom Bilodeau OMI for his listening ear, more recently, Sr. Frances McDougall CND for her mature wisdom in helping me slow down, and my brother Oblate Fr. Al Hubenig, who is graciously serving in that capacity for me now.

Thank you to Lucie Leduc and the staff at Star of the North Retreat Centre in St. Albert for their patience with me and for their moral support. It has been a pleasure to work with Joe Sinasac, Simon Appolloni and Anne Louise Mahoney of Novalis Publishing, who accommodated the extra time I needed to finish the manuscript.

Msgr. Doug Cook and the staff of Our Lady of Mt. Carmel in Newport Beach very generously offered me office space, warm hospitality and a supportive community for a "writing holiday" during which I could also kayak and windsurf. For that I am very grateful.

Lastly, thank you to my family members for always being there for me, my brother bishops for their fellowship, Archbishop Smith and the Archdiocese of Edmonton for their welcome, and my Oblate community for their understanding, encouragement and a place to call home.

Permissions

As indicated in the introduction, much of the material on the second half of life in this book is taken from two main sources: Ron Rolheiser OMI and Richard Rohr OFM. It was difficult to reference much of the material because it came to me in various ways: previously published material, workshops, lectures and retreats I attended that were given by them, personal conversations as well as some online reflections, and my own integration and use of their teachings over the years.

I am very grateful to both these mentors for giving me their permission and blessing, as follows:

I am happy to endorse everything you have written here and attributed to me, and I grant permission to publish this as written, without any further references or specific footnotes to my material. I retain the right, of course, to use this same material in any of my own further writings.

Ron Rolheiser OMI
April 4, 2018

You have my full permission to use quotes and material from my writings and talks in your fine book. I am honored by your trust.

Richard Rohr OFM
April 5, 2018

Select Bibliography

Alighieri, Dante. *The Divine Comedy.* London: Penguin, 1954.

Augustine. *Confessions.* New York: Dover, 2002.

Benedict XVI. Encyclical Letter *Caritatis in Veritate.* Rome: The Vatican, June 29, 2009.

Chittister, Joan. *In Search of Belief.* Liguori, MO: Liguori/Triumph, 1999.

De Chardin, Teilhard. *The Divine Milieu.* New York: Harper Collins, 2001.

De Mello, Anthony. *The Song of the Bird.* New York: Doubleday, 1982.

Dorf, Francis. *The Art of Passing Over.* Mahwah, NJ: Paulist Press, 1988.

Eliot, T.S. *Murder in the Cathedral.* New York: Harcourt Brace, 1935.

Frankl, Victor E. *Man's Search for Meaning.* Boston: Beacon Press, 2006.

Greer, Germaine. *The Change: Women, Aging and Menopause.* New York: Ballantine Books, 1993.

Hassel, David J. *Dark Intimacy.* Mahwah, NJ: Paulist Press, 1986.

Hillman, James. *The Force of Character: And the Lasting Life.* New York: Random House, 1999.

Keating, Thomas. *A Daily Reader for Contemplative Living.* New York: Continuum, 2003.

———. *Open Mind, Open Heart.* New York: Continuum, 1997.

Kübler-Ross, Elisabeth. *On Death and Dying.* New York: Scribner, 1969.

Lavoie, Sylvain. *Walk a New Path.* Toronto: Novalis, 2013.

Martin, James. *My Life with the Saints.* Chicago: Loyola Press, 2007.

Masini, Mario. *Lectio Divina.* Italy: San Paulo, 1996.

Miller, Alice. *The Drama of the Gifted Child: The Search for the True Self.* New York: Basic Books, 2007.

Nouwen, Henri. *With Open Hands.* Notre Dame, IN: Ave Maria Press, 1972.

Pennington, Basil. "The Formation of the False Self and Coming into the True Self." In Richard Rohr and Friends. *Contemplation in Action.* New York: Crossroad, 2006.

Rohr, Richard. *Adam's Return.* New York: Crossroad, 2013.

———. *Breathing Under Water.* Cincinnati: St. Anthony Messenger Press, 2011.

———. *From Wild Man to Wise Man: Reflections on Male Spirituality.* Cincinnati: St. Anthony Messenger Press, 2005.

———. *Immortal Diamond.* San Francisco: Jossey-Bass, 2013.

——— and Friends. *Contemplation in Action.* New York: Crossroad, 2006.

——— with Mike Morrell. *The Divine Dance: The Trinity and Your Transformation.* New Kensington, PA: Whittaker House, 2016.

Rolheiser, Ronald. *Against an Infinite Horizon: The Finger of God in Our Everyday Lives.* New York: Crossroad, 2002.

———. *Sacred Fire.* New York: Image, 2014.

———. *The Holy Longing: The Search for a Christian Spirituality.* New York: Doubleday, 1999.

———. *The Restless Heart: Finding Our Spiritual Home in Times of Loneliness.* New York: Crown, 2006.

Rupp, Joyce. *Praying Our Goodbyes.* Notre Dame, IN: Ave Maria Press, 2012.

Singh, Kathleen Dowling. *The Grace in Aging: Awaken as You Grow Older.* Somerville, MA: Wisdom Publications, 2014.

Vanier, Jean. *Becoming Human.* New York: Paulist Press, 1998.

Viorst, Judith. *Necessary Losses.* New York: The Free Press, 1986.

Young, William P. *The Shack: Where Tragedy Confronts Eternity.* Newberry Park, CA: Windblown Media, 2008.

Endnotes

1 Anthony de Mello SJ, *The Song of the Bird* (New York: Doubleday, 1982), 96.

2 Richard Rohr, Daily Meditations, "True Self and False Self: Week 1," August 6, 2017, https://cac.org/who-am-i-2017-08-06.

3 Irenaeus of Lyons, *Against Heresies, 4:20,7*. See James R. Payton, Jr., *Irenaeus on the Christian Faith: A Condensation of Against Heresies* (Cambridge: James Clarke, 2012), 116.

4 Jean Vanier, *Becoming Human* (New York: Paulist Press, 1998), 40.

5 Benedict XVI, Encyclical Letter *Caritas in Veritate*, 2009, #11.

6 M. Basil Pennington, OCSO, "The Formation of the False Self and Coming into the True Self," in Richard Rohr and Friends, *Contemplation in Action* (New York: Crossroad, 2006), 87–88.

7 Richard Rohr, *Immortal Diamond* (San Francisco: Jossey-Bass, 2013), 3, 4, 16, 22, 23.

8 Richard Rohr, *Breathing Under Water* (New York: Crossroad, 2013), 64.

9 James Martin SJ, *My Life with the Saints* (Chicago: Loyola Press, 2007), 387.

10 Thomas Keating, *Open Mind, Open Heart* (New York: Continuum, 1997), 57.

11 "The dark night of the soul" is the popular phrase used for John of the Cross's overall spiritual paradigm. It is not, in fact, the title of any one of his books, but has become the accepted way of referring to the entire journey he describes. The journey through the "dark night of the soul," for John, has three phases: "the dark night of the senses"; "proficiency"; and "the dark night of the spirit." (See *The Collected Works of St. John of the Cross*, Kieran Kavanaugh OCD, trans. [Washington, DC: ICS Publications, Institute of Carmelite Studies, 1991].) Hence, when you see it written in this text as "the dark night of the spirit," know that in this context, it refers specifically to the final stage of growth and transformation in John of the Cross, as opposed to the overall journey of the soul.

12 Thomas Keating, *The Daily Reader for Contemplative Living* (New York: Continuum, 2003), 9.

13 William Butler Yeats, "Vacillation," Verse IV.

14 From his popular song "Anthem." Here is an unverified quote by Cohen from *The Future Radio Special* (Sony, 1992):

"The future is no excuse for an abdication of your own personal responsibilities towards yourself and your job and your love. 'Ring the bells that still can ring': they're few and far between but you can find them.

"This situation does not admit of solution of perfection. This is not the place where you make things perfect, neither in your marriage, nor in your work, nor anything, nor your love of God, nor your love of family or country. The thing is imperfect.

"And worse, there is a crack in everything that you can put together: Physical objects, mental objects, constructions of any kind. But that's where the light gets in, and that's where the resurrection is and that's where the return, that's where the repentance is. It is with the confrontation, with the brokenness of things."

15   St. Augustine, *Confessions* (Lib 1, 1–2, 2.5, 5: CSEL 33, 1–5).

16   Richard Rohr, *The Divine Dance* (New Kensington, PA: Whittaker House, 2016), 31.

17   Richard Rohr, Daily Meditations, "Interfaith Friendship: Jesus and Buddha," December 8, 2017, https://cac.org/jesus-and-buddha-2017-12-08.

18   Richard Rohr, *Adam's Return* (New York: Crossroad, 2013), 32–33.

19   C.S. Lewis, *The Four Loves*. Adapted from https://www.lib.uidaho.edu/digital/turning/love.html.

20   Judith Viorst, *Necessary Losses* (New York: The Free Press, 1986), 181.

21   St. Gregory, from a sermon: *Oratio* 43, in *Laudem Basilii Magni*, 15, 16–17, 19–21; PG 36, 514–423.

22   Viorst, *Necessary Losses*, 234.

23   David Hassel SJ, *Dark Intimacy: Hope for Those in Difficult Prayer Experiences* (Mahwah, NJ: Paulist Press, 1986), 5.

24   Thomas Moore, *Soul Mates* (Toronto: HarperCollins Canada, 2016), 124.

25   Paul J. Philibert, *The Priesthood of the Faithful: Key to a Living Church* (Collegeville, MN: Liturgical Press, 2005), 109.

26   Martin Luther King, Sermon, Chapter IV, "Love In Action," Atlanta, Georgia, July 1, 1962 – Mar 1, 1963, 176.

27   Richard Rohr, Daily Meditations, "Letting Go: Forgiveness is Letting Go," July 24, 2014, http://conta.cc/1nOY6PH.

28   Joan Chittister, *In Search of Belief* (Liguori, MO: Liguori/Triumph, 1999), 187.

29   Richard Rohr, *From Wild Man to Wise Man* (Cincinnati: St. Anthony Messenger Press, 2005), 83.

30   Viorst, *Necessary Losses*, 325–26.

31   Joyce Rupp, *Praying Our Goodbyes* (Notre Dame, IN: Ave Maria Press, 2012), 55.

32   Richard Rohr, Daily Meditations, "Two Halves of Life: Week 1," June 13, 2016, https://cac.org/entering-dark-wood-2016-06-13.

33   Dante Alighieri, *The Divine Comedy* (London: Penguin, 1954), 16.

34   Jonathan Merritt (ANS Religious News Service, December 5, 2018) describes the Enneagram as "an ancient system of unknown origin with a strange name. It is replete with sacred language, but is not explicitly Christian in orientation. It centers on nine personality types that are arranged into a chart resembling a pentagram.

The Enneagram offers nine mirrors for self-reflection. These nine mirrors, if we choose to gaze into them directly, can help us shake loose of our illusions that end up getting us lost from home in the first place. The Enneagram teaches us nine approaches to observing the patterns of human character structure archetypes. These patterns fortify a kind of psycho-spiritual-somatic muscle memory that shapes how we think, feel, and act."

According to Merritt, in 1990, Franciscan Fr. Richard Rohr effectively Christianized the system for Americans when he published *The Enneagram: A Christian Perspective*. Rohr introduced it to our Oblate community at a retreat years before that book was published. I find it a very effective tool for self-awareness and a key element of personal growth and wellness, along with faith and fellowship. The Jesuits have also worked with and written about the Enneagram.

Unfortunately, some Christians and even some church leaders have taken a negative attitude towards it because of its uncertain origins, described by Merritt as possibly ancient Egypt, pre-historic Korea, Buddhism and Sufi mysticism. He says, "Many Catholic and Protestant scholars claim it was developed by the early church's desert mothers and fathers. We do know that in the 1950s and '60s the Bolivian wisdom teacher Oscar Ichazo brought forward the *Enneagram of Personality*, which is what we commonly use today."

I find it rather puzzling that we can accept, embrace and "Christianize" the thinking of pagan philosophers Plato and Aristotle, pagan symbols like the evergreen tree, and pagan celebrations like that of the return of the sun (the Napateans who flourished in Petra, Jordan, from 100 BC–100 AD celebrated the feast of their main god, Dashara, on December 25), which we have transformed into Christmas, but resist the truth, beauty and goodness found in the Enneagram. It also connects with the Reality Therapy theory of Dr. William Glasser, based on met and unmet needs, as each type expresses a basic human need. I find it fits into our Christian perspective very well, as Jesus is the perfect model of all nine types. Personally, I have found it very helpful (as a number three, my greatest need is to succeed, my greatest fear is failure): Jesus showed me the way as he turned failure into success, crucifixion into resurrection.

35 Francis Dorf, *The Art of Passing Over* (Mahwah, NJ: Paulist Press, 1988). This is a catch-phrase he uses for the book.

36 Jean Vanier, *An Ark for the Poor* (Toronto: Novalis, 2012), 78.

37 Richard Rohr, "Human Development in Scripture," in his *Growing in Love's Likeness* series of daily meditations, March 26, 2018.

38 https://en.wikipedia.org/wiki/Sannyasa

39 During a workshop on how to receive Step Fives that I co-facilitated in North Battleford, Saskatchewan, in the mid-1990s, my co-presenter, the late Fr. Gordon, an Anglican priest who was very experienced in Step Five work, claimed that Jesus had been sexually abused. I was initially shocked upon hearing that statement, but after further reflection, it made sense – that is what prison guards sometime inflict upon the incarcerated under their charge.

As a prisoner himself, Jesus was stripped and flogged. The scriptures remind us that he experienced our suffering and was tested in every way we are, but was without sin (Hebrews 4:15). With the help of that teaching, I came to agree with Gordon's claim. Since then, it has been an invaluable insight to help victims of sexual abuse who cry out, "Where was God when that happened to me?" Just as God did not take away or prevent the pain and suffering of his own Son, so God does not take away or prevent our suffering. Instead, he experiences it with us and in us, and shows us how to bear it in a way that is redemptive, purposeful and meaningful.

40   Richard Rohr, Daily Meditations, "Orthopraxy: Reverse Mission," August 26, 2015, https://cac.org/reverse-mission-2015-08-26.

41   The word "passivities" is clearly not good English, but it is used here as a technical term in opposition to the word "activities." Pierre Teilhard de Chardin uses it widely in his book *The Divine Milieu* to highlight that we do not just help others by what we do for them, that is, through our "activities," but we also, and sometimes even more deeply, help others through what we passively endure, that is, through our "passivities." But the term is also most apt to describe what Jesus gave to us in his death. Jesus gave his life for us through what he actively did for us (his activities), but he gave his death for us through what he endured "passively" for us (his passivities). This is important to highlight because too few Christians understand what is implied when we speak of "the Passion" of Christ. We spontaneously take that to mean the intense "passionate" sufferings he endured. But the word "passion" here needs to be taken in its literal sense, that is, from the Latin *passio*, meaning "passivity." We are saved both through Christ's activities (his ministry) and his passivities (his passive, loving and faith-filled acceptance of his suffering and death).

42   Bill Wilson, "Editorial," *Grapevine* (November 1958).

43   Cited in Edward F. Edinger's *The New God Image: A Study of Jung's Key Letters Concerning the Evolution of the Western God-Image* (Asheville, NC: Chiron Publications, 1997), 162.

44   Ron Rolheiser, "John and Human Development: 'The Dark Night of the Soul'... A Contemporary Interpretation," http://ronrolheiser.com/me/uploads/2014/02/joc_human_dev.pdf.

45   *Our Family* (November 2001). Our Oblate community published this magazine for many years.